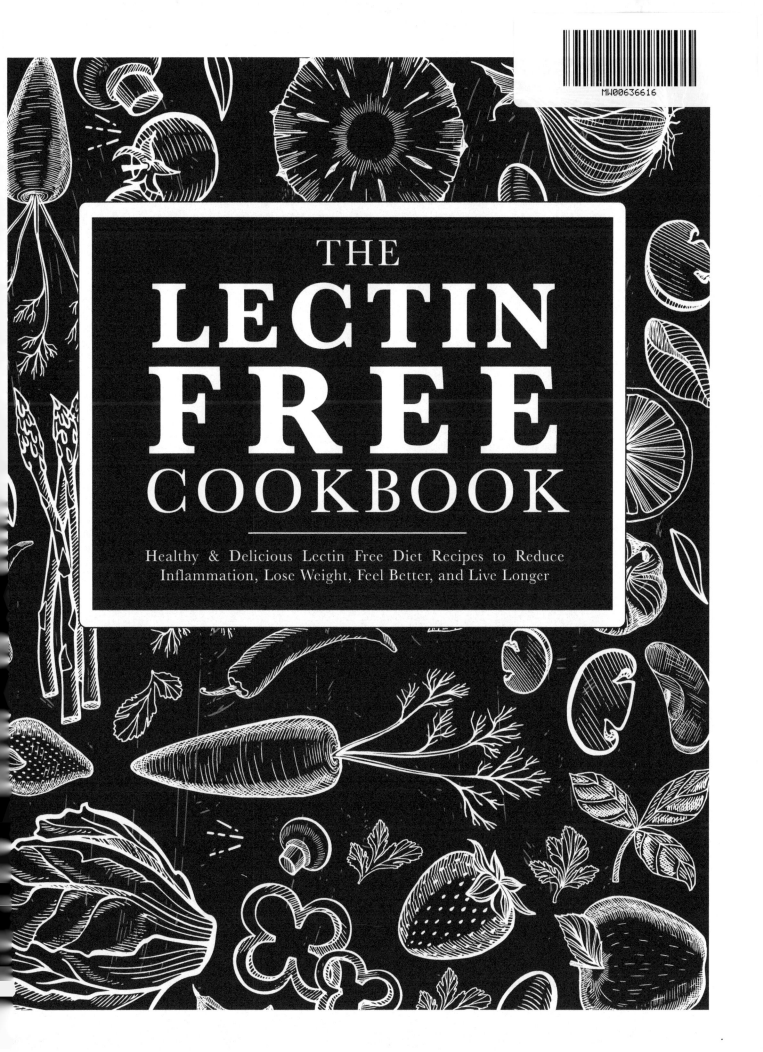

THE
LECTIN
FREE
COOKBOOK

Healthy & Delicious Lectin Free Diet Recipes to Reduce
Inflammation, Lose Weight, Feel Better, and Live Longer

Published in 2018 by
H&L Group

This Book is for informational and educational purposes. Please consult your healthcare provider before beginning any diet or eating program.

WHAT ARE LECTINS?

Lectins are a type of protein that binds carbohydrates in a process known as glycation. Lectins are found in a variety of foods, most notably grains, raw legumes, and nightshade vegetables (egg plant, tomatoes, potatoes, and peppers). Other foods known to contain lectins include: tree nuts (pecans, walnuts, almonds, cashews, and pistachios), gourd family fruits (squash, zucchini, and pumpkin) and dairy products from cows fed corn or soybeans. These proteins are rather sticky and can adhere to cell membranes in various locations within the body. Lectins are not able to be digested. They are resistant to digestive enzymes. The most prominent area of lectin agglutination (clump and stick), is in the intestines. This can cause a host of undesirable issues and will be discussed in the subsequent section. Lectins are also known to induce pro-inflammatory processes which can create systemic disturbances within the body. In addition to their pro-inflammatory characteristics, lectins can also cause nutrient deficiencies and disrupt digestion. But don't worry, there are known methods that reduce lectin content in food items. There is also a host of suitable substitution options that are naturally low in lectins that can constitute any diet to reduce the overall effects associated with lectin intake. These topics will be discussed in the proceeding sections.

GASTROINTESTINAL EFFECTS OF LECTINS

The binding capacity of lectins to cell membranes is an inherent defense mechanism of plants to deter insects and animals. When ingested, lectins commonly bind to the intestinal wall and induce an inflammatory process. Gastrointestinal symptoms that may arise include: abdominal pain, nausea, vomiting, and diarrhea. Internally, lectins not only provoke a pro-inflammatory state, but also reduce the integrity of the intestinal wall. This creates what's known as intestinal permeability in which particles that are normally contained within the intestinal lumen leak through the wall of the intestines. As these contents leak out into circulation, many negative downstream effects can occur. This includes lectin aggregation in individual organs such as the kidneys which may cause localized inflammation and subsequent organ dysfunction. Lectins may also exacerbate preexisting gastrointestinal diseases such as Irritable Bowel Syndrome, Crohn's Disease, Ulcerative Colitis, colon cancer, and Celiac disease.

AUTO-IMMUNE EFFECTS

Lectins have been shown to present as antigens in the human body. An antigen is what the immune system identifies as a foreign body and evokes an immune system response to neutralize the perceived threat. As a result, the immune system creates antibodies that attach to lectins which flags the immune system to attack. This has been shown to result in auto immune responses in multiple organ systems including the pancreas, kidney, and thyroid. By bombarding these organ systems with a misguided attack, organ function is compromised and can end up damaged. The pancreas is responsible for secreting insulin in response to elevated blood sugars. If there is pancreatic dysfunction secondary to an auto immune response, risk of diabetes is enhanced. Similarly, if thyroid dysfunction precipitates as a result of an auto immune response, metabolic rate may be adversely affected. Considering the known affects of lectins and immune system provocation, lectins have also been hypothesized to play a central role in rheumatoid arthritis (RA). RA is characterized as a chronic auto-inflammatory condition that adversely affects many joints, including those in the hands and feet. RA can result in joint swelling, erosion, and deformity.

NUTRIENT ABSORPTION

Nutrients in the diet are largely absorbed in the small intestine. The small intestine is approximately 5 feet long to increase the surface area and ultimately the absorptive capacity of nutrients. Some surgeries requiring removal of portions of the intestines or bypassing certain sections can reduce absorption of micronutrients leading to deficiency symptoms. When lectins are consumed and adhere to the intestinal wall, the surface area is reduced. This concept is similar to the aforementioned surgical procedures. Additionally, lectin agglutination on the intestinal wall can also cause damage which further reduces absorption. Nutrient deficiencies secondary to these mechanisms can lead to serious symptoms including but not limited to: anemia, osteoporosis, neuropathy (nerve dysfunction), alopecia (hair loss), malnutrition, and increased susceptibility to infections. Lectins can also negatively impact the gut bacteria which is necessary for proper immune system function and vitamin synthesis. Gut bacteria also aid in the absorption of certain minerals such as calcium, iron, and magnesium. Reducing lectin intake can dramatically enhance nutrient absorption in those suffering from lectin induced malabsorptive issues.

METHODS TO REDUCE LECTIN CONTENT

There are many foods that contain high amounts of lectins. However, there are steps that can be taken to significantly reduce lectin levels. Using moist heat is beneficial to reduce lectin levels. Using a slow cooker is not ideal as the temperature does not reach a high enough temp to effectively eliminate lectins. Other known methods of reducing lectins levels include: fermenting, boiling, sprouting, peeling, pressure cooking, and deseeding. Grains and legumes should be soaked, preferably in a baking soda bath overnight. The soak water should be replaced multiple times to ensure adequate disposal of the lectins that have leeched into the water. To most effectively reduce the amount of lectins in any particular food item, using multiple preparation methods for each item is ideal.

FOODS ALLOWED

The following foods contain very little or no lectins and are therefore OK to consume regularly.

- Cricket flour
- Hemp protein
- Fish (wild caught)
- Beef (grass fed)
- Chicken
- Coconut flour
- Pork
- Liver
- Bone broth
- Eggs (pasture raised, fed NON-soy feed)
- Brewers or nutritional yeast
- Raw honey (limited, and only for some people)
- Extra virgin olive oil
- Ghee
- Avocado oil
- Leafy greens (spinach, bok choy, collard greens, etc.)
- Cruciferous vegetables: broccoli, cauliflower, kale, Brussels sprouts
- Fruits: mango, citrus, pineapple, blueberries, apples
- Onions
- Mushrooms
- Sweet potatoes
- Celery

Listed below are foods with high lectin levels (left) and similar alternatives with lower lectin levels (right). Recommend using cooking/ prep methods to further reduce lectin levels.

Beans, lentils, peas, peanuts	→ Rice beans, cowpeas, broad beans, lupin seeds
Squash, zucchini, pumpkin	→ Cucumber, Okra, Daikon radish, Beets
Eggplant, peppers, potatoes, and tomatoes	→ Japanese sweet potato, Turnips, Jicama
Grains (wheat, barley, rye, oats, ancient grains)	→ Coconut flour, almond flour, cauliflower rice
Dairy products from corn/soybean-fed cows	→ Grass fed dairy, goat cheese/butter, coconut yogurt, goat & sheep kefir
Tree Nuts	→ Hemp seeds, psyllium
Yeast (except brewer and nutritional)	→ Brewers and nutrition yeast

LOW LECTIN
CONTAINING SNACKS

- Siete Grain Free Tortilla Chips
- 1 ounce of extra dark chocolate (72% cacao or more)
- Sweet potato hummus (tahini free) with celery
- Sweet potato chips
- Kale chips
- Coconut yogurt
- Sweet potato fries
- Cauliflower rice cakes
- Baby carrots

FOODS TO AVOID

The following food items contain higher amounts of lectins and should be limited or avoided. The food preparation methods listed above can be used to reduce lectin content if the food item is to be consumed.

- Beans, lentils, peas, and peanuts
- Squash, zucchini, pumpkin
- Eggplant, peppers, potatoes, and tomatoes
- Grains (wheat, barley, rye, oats, ancient grains)
- Dairy products from cows fed corn or soybeans
- Tree Nuts
- Yeast (except brewer and nutritional)

IN CONCLUSION

It is known that lectins can cause gastrointestinal discomfort and result in GI symptoms. Furthermore, lectins may bind to the intestinal wall and induce leaky gut in which particles leak through causing downstream inflammatory processes in other organ systems such as the kidneys, thyroid, and pancreas. Lectins may also exacerbate symptoms associated with Rheumatoid Arthritis. Normal micronutrient absorption may also be compromised upon lectin intake as these proteins can cause intestinal damage and diminish absorptive capacity causing nutrient deficiency symptoms. The deleterious effects of these lectins can be reduced by deploying cooking/preparation methods known to effectively decrease lectin level concentrations. When using multiple methods per high lectin food item, you can significantly reduce the downstream consequences of lectin intake. Lastly, to reduce lectin intake most markedly, simply choose foods that contain very little to no lectin as listed above.

I hope you enjoy the following registered dietitian-created recipes!

BREAKFAST

SIDES, SNACKS, & ENTREES

DESSERT

STICKY CINNAMON BUNS

Prep time: 15 mins • **Cook time: 25 mins** • **12 Buns**

INGREDIENTS

For the Dough

- 2 tsp xanthan gum
- 3 ½ - 4 cups all purpose gluten-free flour
- 2 ½ tsp baking powder
- ¼ tsp salt
- ½ cup Swerve
- 6 Tbsp unsalted butter, at room temperature
- 2 eggs at room temperature, lightly beaten
- 1 cup coconut milk, at room temperature
- Unflavored dental floss (to cut the dough, not to eat)

For the Filling

- 2 Tbsp ground cinnamon
- 1 cup Stevia brown sugar
- 1/8 tsp salt
- 4 Tbsp unsalted butter, melted and cooled

For the Glaze

- 1 Tbsp coconut milk, plus more by the ¼ tsp if necessary
- 2 packets Stevia + 1 cup arrowroot, mixed with food processor

1. Preheat oven to 350°F.

2. Grease a twelve-cup muffin tin and set aside.

3. In a large bowl, mix the flour, xanthan gum, baking powder, ¼ tsp of the salt, and the Swerve.

4. Add 6 Tbsp butter, eggs, and 1 cup milk, and mix until the dough comes together. If the dough seems sticky, add more flour by the tablespoon and knead it in with well-floured hands until the dough is smooth.

5. Lightly dust your clean countertop with flour and place dough on top. Sprinkle the dough lightly with extra flour and roll it into a 12-inch by 15-inch rectangle, about 1/4 inch thick (no thinner).

6. For the filling: In a medium-size bowl, mix together the brown sugar, cinnamon, 1/8 tsp salt, and 4 tbsp butter (melted and cooled).

7. Use a large spoon or spatula to spread the filling in an even layer over the top of the dough, leaving about 1/4 inch clean around the perimeter.

8. Start at one end of the dough and roll the dough away from you into a tightly formed roll.

9. Use dental floss (unflavored) to slice by doing the following: hold ends of floss in each hand, slide floss under the dough about an inch from the end. Cross the floss and pull the floss away from the dough, allowing it to cut through the roll. Continue doing this until you have twelve 1 inch thick rolls. Place each roll in the greased muffin tin.

10. Place the tin in the center of the preheated oven, and bake for about 25 minutes, or until the rolls begin to turn golden brown. Remove from the oven and let cool until the rolls are firm enough to handle (approx. 10 minutes), then transfer to a cooling rack. Be sure to remove the rolls from the muffin tin before they are completely cool, or they will begin to stick to the muffin tin.

11. Prepare the icing while the rolls are cooling: in a small bowl, combine the Stevia and arrowroot mixture with 1 tablespoon of coconut milk. Mix well until a thick paste forms. Add more milk by the 1/4-teaspoon if needed. Add milk very slowly, as it is much easier to thin, than to thicken, the glaze (add more of the arrowroot/Stevia mixture if too thin). You want the glaze to be thick, but thin enough to drip off of the spoon.

12. Drizzle glaze over top of the cinnamon rolls.

JICAMA HASH BROWNS

Prep time: 10 mins • **Cook time: 15 mins** • **4 Servings**

INGREDIENTS

- 1 Jicama, peeled and grated
- ½ yellow onion, finely chopped
- 2 garlic cloves, minced
- 2 eggs
- 1 Tbsp coconut oil
- ½ tsp paprika
- Salt and pepper to taste

1. In a large nonstick skillet, add coconut oil. Heat until melted.

2. Add the garlic and onion. Cook over medium heat until translucent.

3. In a medium bowl, whisk together eggs and paprika. Add jicama to egg mixture and mix until combined, then add to hot skillet.

4. Turn heat up to medium. Cook for 5 minutes or until golden brown. Flip bottom side to top and cook another 5 minutes on medium high heat.

5. Serve as a side to your favorite breakfast items!

ALMOND FLOUR BISCUITS

Prep time: 10 mins • **Cook time: 15 mins** • **12 Biscuits**

INGREDIENTS

- 1 cup almond flour
- 1 cup coconut flour
- 2 tsp baking powder
- 1/2 tsp salt
- 2 large eggs, beaten
- 1/3 cup ghee butter

1. Preheat the oven to 350 degrees F.

2. Line a baking sheet with parchment paper.

3. In a large bowl, mix together the flour, baking powder, and salt.

4. Stir in Beaten eggs and ghee.

5. Scoop dough (approx. 1 Tbsp) onto your baking sheet. Flatten slightly.

6. Bake for 15 minutes, or until golden brown.

7. Cool on baking sheet.

8. Serve with your favorite dish and enjoy!

TEMPEH BACON AND EGG BREAKFAST SANDWICH

Prep time: 10 mins • Cook time: 40 mins • 4 Servings

INGREDIENTS FOR BISCUITS

- ¾ cup almond flour (NOT almond meal)
- ¾ cup coconut flour
- 1 tsp baking powder
- ½ tsp salt
- 3 Tbsp ghee butter, diced small
- 3 Tbsp coconut cream
- 1 egg

INGREDIENTS FOR BACON

- 8oz grain-free tempeh, thinly sliced
- 3 Tbsp coconut aminos
- 1 Tbsp extra virgin olive oil
- 1 Tbsp rice wine vinegar
- ¼ tsp sea salt
- 1 tsp smoked paprika
- ¼ tsp black pepper
- 1 tsp chipotle powder
- 5 drops liquid stevia
- ¼ tsp liquid smoke

DIRECTIONS FOR BISCUITS

1. Preheat oven to 350 degrees F.

2. Take a cookie sheet and line with parchment paper, and set aside.

3. In a medium bowl, combine flour, baking powder, and salt.

4. Add diced butter and cut into the flour, using a pastry cutter or butter knife. Keep cutting the butter into smaller pieces, and pressing into the flour until all the chunks are gone and the dough is crumbly.

5. Make a space in the middle of the bowl, and crack in an egg and add the cream. Use a fork to lightly mix the egg and cream together, slowly incorporating the rest of the dough. Mix until the dough is soft.

6. Using your hands, divide dough into four pieces and roll into a ball. Dough will be soft and slightly sticky.

7. Place dough balls onto parchment lined cookie sheet. DO NOT flatten dough.

8. Bake for 20 minutes or until lightly golden.

9. Let cool slightly before slicing.

DIRECTIONS FOR BACON

1. In a small bowl, whisk coconut aminos, rice wine vinegar, sea salt, chipotle powder, pepper, paprika, black pepper, liquid smoke, and liquid stevia together.

2. Add tempeh slices to mixture and flip to coat all sides. Let sit to marinate, approx. 5 minutes.

3. In a large skillet, heat 1 Tbsp olive oil over medium heat.

4. Once tempeh IS done marinating, add to hot skillet. NOTE: may need to do this in several batches in order to not crowd the pan.

5. Cook for 3-4 minutes, browning each side. Be careful because these can burn quickly!

6. Add extra oil to pan if needed.

Additional items:
- 4 eggs (cooked over-easy)
- 1 avocado, pitted, slice, peeled
- 4 slices mozzarella cheese

Assembly of sandwich:
- Slice biscuits in half, smash avocado on one half of biscuit and layer overeasy egg and mozzarella cheese.

BANANA NUT PANCAKES

Prep time: 10 mins • Cook time: 15 mins • 1 Serving

INGREDIENTS

- 1 ½ large ripe bananas
- 2 eggs
- 1/8 teaspoon baking powder
- 1 Tbsp ghee butter
- Toppings: whipped coconut cream (see recipe below),
  sugar-free maple syrup, hazelnut butter, chopped walnuts

DIRECTIONS

1. In a mixing bowl, whisk together the eggs and baking powder.

2. In another bowl, mash 1 ½ bananas with a potato masher or a fork. Do not over mash, there should be chunks of bananas.

3. Pour wet mixture into mashed bananas and stir to combine.

4. In a frying pan, heat ghee butter over medium-low heat. Once hot, scoop out pancake mixture and place in pan (can be as big or as small of an amount as you want).

5. Once the pan side down is golden brown, flip the pancake(s) and cook for about one minute more.

6. Place the pancake(s) on a plate and spread hazelnut butter on top. Sprinkle a layer of chopped walnuts and then place dollop of your whipped coconut cream on top.

7. Drizzle with sugar-free maple syrup.

8. Enjoy!

CINNAMON COCONUT FLOUR PANCAKES

Prep time: 10 mins • **Cook time: 5 mins** • **4 Servings**

INGREDIENTS

- ¼ cup coconut flour
- 1/8 cup arrowroot powder
- ½ tsp baking soda
- 2 eggs, room temperature
- 2 Tbsp coconut oil, melted
- ¼ cup light coconut milk
- 1/8 – ¼ tsp cinnamon
- ¼ cup strawberries, washed and diced
- ½ Tbsp pure maple syrup

1. In a small bowl, whisk together arrowroot flour, cinnamon, coconut flour, baking soda, and salt until thoroughly combined.

2. In a medium bowl mix eggs, coconut milk, and coconut oil together. Add dry mixture and mix until well combined.

3. Let batter sit for approx 3-5 minutes (this will allow batter to thicken). While batter is setting, heat a pan (lightly greased) on medium heat.

4. Place 2 Tbsp of batter onto hot pan, spreading the batter out a little. Cook for approx. 3 minutes before flipping. Cook each side until lightly browned.

5. Serve hot with strawberries and pure maple syrup on top!

PEACHY KEEN PANCAKES

Prep time: 10 mins • **Cook time: 30 mins** • **4 Servings**

INGREDIENTS

- 2 large eggs
- 1 tsp pure vanilla extract
- 5 oz plain goat's milk kefir
- 1 Tbsp coconut oil, melted
- ¼ cup coconut flour
- ¼ cup tapioca flour
- ¼ cup almond flour

- ¼ tsp sea salt
- ½ tsp baking powder
- ¼ tsp baking soda
- 2 ripe peaches, peeled and cut into thin slices
- Shredded coconut
- 1 Tbsp pure maple syrup
- ½ tsp cinnamon

1. Preheat oven to 350 degrees F.

2. Oil an 8-inch pie pan with coconut oil.

3. Beat together eggs, vanilla extract, and kefir. Slowly add the coconut oil, whisking constantly so the oil doesn't solidify.

4. Add the coconut flour, tapioca flour, almond flour, sea salt, baking soda, and baking powder. Whisk together until batter is smooth.

5. Pour the batter into the pie pan. Place half of the peach slices on top of the batter in a single layer.

6. Bake for 30 minutes, testing with a toothpick until it comes out clean. Let the pancake cool to room temperature before slicing.

7. Top with the remaining peach slices, sprinkle with cinnamon and toasted shredded coconut, and pure maple syrup.

NOTE: you do not have to make one big pancake, you can scoop small batches of pancake batter onto hot skillet. Flip as each side browns.

BREAKFAST SWEET POTATO MASH

Prep time: 10 mins • Cook time: 5 mins • 1-2 Servings

INGREDIENTS

- 1 sweet potato, washed and peeled
- 1/3 cup crushed ripe banana (about 1 medium banana)
- ¼ cup coconut milk
- ½ tsp cinnamon
- ¼ tsp nutmeg
- Pinch of salt
- 1 banana, mashed
- Handful of chopped walnuts
- 1 Tbsp almond butter

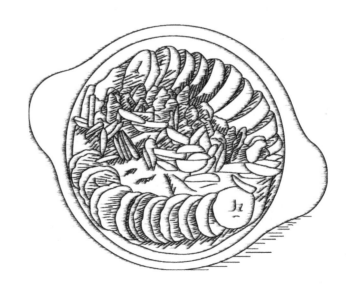

1. Place the shredder attachment to a food processor. Run the sweet potato through it.

2. Switch to the blade attachment and pulse the sweet potato several times, until lumpy.

3. In a medium microwave safe bowl, combine the mashed sweet potato, banana, coconut milk, cinnamon, nutmeg, and salt. Microwave for approx. 3 minutes, or until cooked.

4. Carefully remove from microwave and top with sliced banana, chopped walnuts, and a hearty drizzle of almond butter.

5. Enjoy!

ANGEL HAIR PASTA WITH CHICKEN AND AVOCADO

Prep time: 10-15 mins • **Cook time: 35 mins** • **6 Servings**

INGREDIENTS

- 2 chicken breasts, boneless, skinless
- 2 Tbsp ghee butter
- 2 packs of Shirataki noodles
- ¼ cup coconut oil
- 2 avocados, pitted and peeled
- 2 Tbsp lime juice
- Salt and pepper to taste

1. Heat skillet over medium heat, add 2 Tbsp ghee butter. Once hot, place chicken breast in pan and cook each side for approx. 10 minutes. When time is up, check internal temp and make sure it is 165 degrees F. Remove from stove. NOTE: you can prepare chicken with seasonings of your choice.

2. While chicken is cooking, prepare noodles: add water to a pot and bring to boil. While water is coming to a boil, drain the Shirataki noodles from their package by adding them to a strainer, rinse well with running water.

3. Transfer noodles to boiling water and cook for approx. 2-3 minutes.

4. Drain the noodles again and place in a hot skillet (no oil, liquid, or any other ingredients). Fry over medium heat for 10 minutes to remove excess water, but do not let them dry out. Using tongs is the easiest way to move the noodles around in the pan.

5. When noodles are done, add them to a bowl with the cooked chicken (you can either dice or shred the chicken).

6. For the sauce, add coconut oil, avocado, lime juice, salt, and pepper in a high powered blender, blend until smooth.

7. Add sauce to noodles and chicken, gently tossing until thoroughly combined.

8. Top with cilantro, parsley, or a bit of sriracha and enjoy!

CAULIFLOWER FETA MEATBALLS WITH SEASONED CHICKEN

Prep time: 1.5 hours • Cook time: 1 hour • 4 Servings

INGREDIENTS

For the Chicken

- 4 chicken breasts, boneless and skinless, pasture-raised
- 2-3 Tbsp ghee butter
- Sea salt and lemon pepper to taste

For the Meatballs

- ½ Head cauliflower, washed, cored, cut into florets
- ½ cup Feta cheese
- 1 lemon rind and juice
- ½ Tbsp garlic powder
- 2 Tbsp fresh parsley, finely chopped
- 2 Tbsp olive oil

1. Place cauliflower in a food processor or blender and pulse until it is like the consistency of rice.

2. Heat a frying pan over medium heat and add olive oil.

3. Once hot, add cauliflower rice and sauté for 5-7 minutes.

4. Remove from heat and place in a large bowl.

5. Add crumbled feta, lemon juice/rind, salt, pepper, garlic powder, and parsley, mix everything together thoroughly.

6. Shape the mixture into small balls and place on a cookie sheet lined with parchment paper.

7. Place in refrigerator to set for 1 hour (optional, but highly recommended).

8. When the hour is almost up, preheat the oven to 375 degrees F and bake the cauliflower meatballs for 10 minutes, then turn them and bake for another 10 minutes.

9. While meatballs are cooking, follow the next step for cooking the chicken.

10. First, flatten the chicken breasts with a meat tenderizer, pound until even in thickness.

11. Season all sides of the chicken breast with salt and lemon pepper.

12. Heat 3 Tbsp ghee butter in a large skillet on medium heat.

13. Once pan is hot and butter is melted, add chicken breasts. Cook 2 minute and turn the heat to medium-low and flip chicken.

14. Cover skillet with lid and cook without uncovering for 12 minutes.

15. Turn off the stove, keep skillet on stove top without removing lid, and let sit for an additional 6-8 minutes.

16. Once time is up, check the internal temperature of the chicken to ensure that it is 165 degrees F.

17. Now, you are ready to serve!

CAULIFLOWER GRILLED CHEESEAND AVOCADO

Prep time: 5-10 mins • **Cook time: 20 mins** • **2 Servings**

INGREDIENTS

- 1 medium head of cauliflower, washed and cored
- 1 large egg
- ½ cup shredded Parmesan cheese
- 1 tsp Italian seasoning
- 4 slices mozzarella cheese
- ½ avocado, pitted, peeled, sliced
- ¼ cup goat cheese, crumbled

1. Preheat oven to 450F.

2. Place cauliflower into food processor and pulse until crumbs about half the size of a grain of rice.

3. Place cauliflower crumbs into a large microwave safe bowl and microwave for 2 minutes. Your cauliflower should be soft and tender.

4. Stir cauliflower and place back into the microwave and cook for another 3 minutes.

5. Remove and stir again so that all the cauliflower cooks evenly. Place back into microwave and cook for 5 minutes. At this point, you should see the cauliflower is becoming drier.

6. Mix again and microwave for another 5 minutes. Cauliflower should still be slightly moist to the touch, but should look dry and clumped.

7. Allow cauliflower to cool for a few minutes. Then add in egg, Parmesan cheese, and seasoning, stir to combine until smooth paste forms.

8. Divide dough into 4 equal parts. Place onto large baking sheet lined with parchment paper. Using your knuckles and fingers, shape into square bread slices about 1/3 inch thick.

9. Bake cauliflower "bread" for about 15 minutes or until slightly golden brown. Remove from oven and let cool a few minutes.

10. Using a spatula, carefully slide cauliflower bread off of parchment paper and assemble your grilled cheese sandwich: layer avocado slices and cheeses onto cauliflower "bread".

11. Heat a pan over medium heat and add ghee butter. Once hot, cook sandwich until cheese is melted and the cauliflower is crispy. You can also bake the sandwiches in the oven.

CHICKEN AND MUSHROOM "RISOTTO"

Prep time: 15 mins • Cook time: 25 mins • 4 Servings

INGREDIENTS

- ½ - ¾ lb boneless, skinless chicken breast
- 2 oz bacon
- 2 Tbsp ghee butter
- 1 large head cauliflower, washed, cored, cut into large chunks
- 1 large yellow onion, diced
- 2 cloves garlic, minced
- ¾ lb mushrooms, thinly sliced
- ½ cup bone broth
- Salt and pepper to taste

1. Heat 1 tsp oil in a pot or skillet over high heat. Add bacon and cook until golden. Transfer to small microwave-proof bowl.

2. Leave about 1 Tbsp bacon fat in pot - discard excess. Add chicken and cook until thoroughly cooked, transfer to a separate bowl.

3. Process cauliflower florets in a food processor or blender until a "rice like" texture.

4. In a large skillet, melt butter over medium heat and sauté onions until caramelized, then add garlic and mushrooms. Sauté mushrooms until brown on both sides.

5. Add the cauliflower rice and broth and turn heat to low. Allow cauliflower to soak up the broth (approx. 10 minutes – don't allow to get too mushy).

6. Add cooked chicken and bacon and warm thoroughly.

7. Add salt and pepper to taste.

8. Serve and enjoy!

CHICKEN, APPLE, AND SHAVED BRUSSELS SPROUT SALAD

Prep time: 30 mins • Cook time: 25 mins • 6 Servings

INGREDIENTS FOR CHICKEN

- 4 chicken breasts, boneless and skinless
- 2-3 Tbsp ghee butter
- Sea salt and lemon pepper to taste

INGREDIENTS FOR SALAD

- ¾ lb Brussels sprouts, shredded
- 3 cups red cabbage, shredded
- 1 large apple, cut and chopped
- ¼ cup extra virgin olive oil

- 1 Tbsp raw honey
- 1 Tbsp mustard
- 1 Tbsp apple cider vinegar
- Salt and pepper to taste

DIRECTIONS FOR SALAD

1. To shred the Brussels sprouts, start by cutting off the hard stem and remove any outer damaged leaves. Then place in a food processor using the thin slicing blade (can do this with the red cabbage as well). If you do not have a food processor, then shred them using a knife by cutting them in half, lengthwise, and then shred as thin as possible.

2. Core the apple, cut into slices and then dice to a size of your preference.

3. Add shredded Brussels sprouts and cabbage, diced apple, and cooked chicken to a bowl.

4. For the dressing: whisk together the mustard, vinegar, olive oil, honey, and salt in a small bowl.

5. Pour the dressing over salad and toss to combine evenly. Serve and enjoy!

DIRECTIONS FOR CHICKEN

1. First, flatten the chicken breasts with a meat tenderizer, pound until even in thickness.

2. Season all sides of the breast with salt and lemon pepper.

3. Heat 3 Tbsp ghee butter in a large skillet on medium heat.

4. Once pan is hot and butter is melted, add chicken breasts. Cook 2 minute and turn the heat to medium-low and flip chicken.

5. Cover skillet with lid and cook without uncovering for 12 minutes.

6. Turn off the stove, keep skillet on stove-top without removing lid. Let sit for an additional 6-8 minutes.

7. Once time is up, check the internal temperature of the chicken to ensure that it is 165 degrees F.

8. Dice or shred the chicken and add to salad.

CREAMY ARTICHOKE PASTRY

Prep time: 1.5 hours • Cook time: 1 hour • 16 Servings

INGREDIENTS

For the filling

- 1 Tbsp olive oil
- 1 garlic clove, crushed
- 1 can (8.5 oz) artichoke hearts, drained and cut in half
- 1 small bunch of fresh Italian parsley, chopped
- 1 tsp of thyme
- 2 eggs
- ¼ cup heavy cream
- 5 oz Fontina cheese (or other mild cheese), cubed
- ½ cup Parmesan cheese, grated
- Salt and pepper to taste

For the Crust

- ¾ cup coconut flour
- ¾ cup almond flour
- ½ tsp salt
- 4oz ghee butter, cold, cut into small cubes
- 6 Tbsp chilled water

1. In a food processor or mixer, add the flour and salt. Pulse a couple of times to mix.

2. Add the butter and pulse a few more times until you get small, pea-sized clumps.

3. Add about 4 Tbsp of chilled water. Pulse only a few times, and check the dough. You may need to add a little more water if necessary. If so, pulse again and then make sure to stop as soon as the dough comes together in a ball.

4. Form into a disc shape, wrap in plastic wrap and refrigerate for one hour or longer.

5. Preheat the oven to 375° F (190° C).

6. Remove the dough from refrigerator and roll it flat on a lightly flour dusted clean surface. Make it into a rectangle, about 2 inches bigger than your pan.

7. Grease the pan with butter and flour, and transfer the dough to the pan. Be careful not to stretch the dough. Make a thick edge that hangs a little off the edge of the pan, trimming off any excess dough. Prick the bottom of the crust sporadically with a fork.

8. Cover dough with parchment paper and then pour baking weights (or dry beans) onto paper.

9. Blind bake for 15 minutes at 375° F (190° C).

10. While the crust is baking, prepare the filling with the following steps: in a large pan, heat one tablespoon of olive oil. Once pan is hot, add the garlic and sauté for a few minutes. Add the artichoke hearts and cook for an additional 5-10 minutes or until soft.

11. Add the chopped parsley and thyme, mix well.

12. In a medium bowl, whisk the eggs, heavy cream, salt and pepper.

13. When the oven timer goes off for the crust, remove from the oven, and remove the parchment paper with the weights.

14. Arrange the artichokes on top of the crust.

15. Pour the egg mixture over the artichokes and then add the fontina cheese and sprinkle with Parmesan cheese.

16. Bake for an additional 25-30 minutes, until golden and softly set.

17. Cut in slices or triangles and serve.

CRISPY BAKED MUSHROOMS

Prep time: 10 mins • **Cook time: 20 mins** • **6 Servings**

INGREDIENTS

- ¼ cup coconut flour
- ¼ cup tapioca flour
- ½ cup nutritional yeast
- ½ tsp cayenne pepper, ground
- ½ tsp garlic powder
- Salt and pepper to taste
- 2 cups baby bella mushrooms, sliced and stems removed
- 1 cup unsweetened coconut milk

44

1. Preheat oven to 425 degrees F.

2. In a small bowl, combine both flours, cayenne pepper, salt, pepper, nutritional yeast, and garlic powder.

3. Toss sliced mushrooms in milk, then use a fork to remove from bowl (let The excess drip off), then toss them in the bowl with the seasoning mixture until covered.

4. Transfer the mushrooms onto a baking sheet lined with parchment paper, make sure they are not clumped together.

5. Bake for 10 minutes, then flip mushrooms, and bake again for another 10 minutes.

6. Remove and serve immediately. Enjoy!

CURRY CAULIFLOWER

Prep time: 10 mins • **Cook time: 35 mins** • **8 Servings**

INGREDIENTS

- 2 cloves garlic, minced
- 2 Tbsp coconut oil
- 4 cups cauliflower florets
- 2 cups light coconut milk, canned
- 1 ½ tsp curry powder
- Salt and pepper to taste

DIRECTIONS

1. Preheat oven to 375 degrees F.

2. In a small skillet, place oil and garlic in pan and sauté over medium heat for 1-2 minutes.

3. Mix coconut milk, salt, pepper, and curry powder together. Then add garlic and oil, mix until combined.

4. Place cauliflower in a casserole dish and pour liquid mixture over cauliflower.

5. Bake for 25-30 minutes.

6. Enjoy!

EGG ROLL BOWL

Prep time: 5 mins • **Cook time: 20-25 mins** • **4 Servings**

INGREDIENTS

- 2 Tbsp avocado oil
- 6 scallions, sliced, green and white parts divided
- ½ cup red onion, diced
- 5 cloves garlic, minced
- 1 lb ground chicken
- 1 tsp fresh, grated ginger
- 2-3 Tbsp sriracha
- 14 ounce bag coleslaw mix
- 3 Tbsp coconut aminos
- 1 Tbsp rice wine vinegar
- Salt and pepper to taste
- ¼ cup mayonnaise (avocado and oil based)

1. Pour oil into large skillet and place over medium heat.

2. Add white parts of green onions, diced red onion, and garlic. Sauté, stirring frequently until red onion begins to soften (approx. 5 minutes).

3. Add ground chicken, grated ginger, and 1 tablespoon sriracha and cook until chicken is browned, broken up, and cooked through (approx. 7-10 minutes).

4. Add coleslaw mix, coconut aminos, rice wine vinegar, and salt and pepper to taste.

5. Stir until well combined.

6. Continue to cook, stirring regularly, until cabbage is tender (approx. 5 minutes).

7. Meanwhile, in a small bowl whisk together ¼ cup mayonnaise and 1-2 tablespoons sriracha. Add a pinch of salt, to taste.

8. To plate: spoon a hearty helping of the chicken-cabbage mixture in a serving bowl. Snip off the corner of the sandwich bag with the creamy chili sauce and drizzle over mixture.

9. Garnish with green parts of the green onions and enjoy!

LEMON SALMON PATTIES

Prep time: 15-20 mins   •   Cook time: 1 hour or more   •   4 Servings

INGREDIENTS FOR PATTIES

- 2 ¼ cups (12 oz) cooked salmon, flaked
- ¼ cup mashed sweet potatoes (see below)
- 4 scallions, chopped
- 1 Tbsp fresh parsley, chopped
- 1 Tbsp Dijon mustard

- 1 Tbsp lemon juice
- 1 egg beaten
- ¾ tsp salt
- ½ tsp ground black pepper

INGREDIENTS FOR AIOLI

- 1 egg yolk
- 1 Tbsp fresh lemon juice
- ½ tsp Dijon mustard

- ½ cup EVOO
- 1 large clove garlic
- 1 tsp fresh dill, copped

DIRECTIONS FOR PATTIES

1. To make mashed sweet potatoes: peel and chop 1 large sweet potato and place the chopped pieces in a small pan. Cover the potatoes in 1 inch of water and bring to a boil on high heat. Reduce the temperature to let simmer and cover. Let heat for 15 minutes or until you can easily pierce the potatoes with a fork. Drain the potatoes, place in bowl, and mash with a fork .

2. Preheat oven to 350 degrees F.

3. In a large mixing bowl, add all of the salmon cake ingredients and mix everything together with a fork until combined.

4. Form mini patties, about 3 inches in diameter, and place on a baking sheet.

5. Bake for 25-30 minutes or until firm and browned on the sides. *Make sure to flip the patties over in the oven halfway through cook time.

DIRECTIONS FOR AIOLI

1. While salmon cakes are baking make the aioli.

2. Place the egg yolk, ½ Tbsp lemon juice, and mustard in a small bowl or blender/processor.

3. Start whisking/blending (easiest with an immersion blender) everything together until the mixture thickens.

4. Then gradually pour in the olive oil while continuing to blend. Please keep in mind that it is important to add the oil slowly because adding too much too soon will result in a runny aioli.

5. You are aiming for a thick, creamy texture.

6. Add the remaining lemon juice along with the garlic and dill and mix in by hand.

7. Taste and season with salt if needed.

8. Transfer the aioli to a small bowl and serve with the salmon cakes.

PORTOBELLO MUSHROOM PIZZAS

Prep time: 15-20 mins • Cook time: 1 hour • 2 Servings

(this includes making your own sauce)

INGREDIENTS FOR PIZZA

- 2 Large Portobello mushrooms, stems removed
- 1-2 Tbsp extra virgin olive oil
- 6 Tbsp homemade marinara sauce (see below)
- 2 slices prosciutto
- 4 slices mozzarella cheese
- Salt and pepper to taste

INGREDIENTS FOR MARINARA SAUCE

- 1 Tbsp coconut oil
- 1 yellow onion, chopped
- 2 garlic cloves, minced
- ½ lb carrots, chopped
- 1 medium beet, chopped
- 1 cup water
- 1 tsp salt
- Pepper to taste

DIRECTIONS FOR PIZZA

1. If you have a grill: set one burner on high. If you do not have a grill: place a grill pan on the stove with burner on high.

2. Rub the top cap of the mushrooms with olive oil, place on grill/grill pan with the cap side up and cook for approx. 4-5 minutes.

3. Flip mushrooms over (so the "gill" side is up) and cook for another 5 minutes.

4. Remove the mushrooms from the pan/grill, but leave the heat on.

5. For each mushroom, add 3 Tbsp marinara sauce into the gill side of the mushroom, 1 slice of prosciutto, and then top with 2 slices of mozzarella cheese.

6. Return to the heat and cook for another 5 minutes or until cheese is melted.

7. Season to taste and enjoy!

DIRECTIONS FOR MARINARA SAUCE

1. Place a large pot on the stove and turn heat to medium, add coconut oil.

2. Once coconut oil melted, add onions and sauté until tender and lightly golden.

3. Add minced garlic and sauté for 1-2 minutes.

4. Add carrots, water, and beets and bring to a boil.

5. Cover and lower heat to a simmer, cooking until beets and carrots are tender when poked with a fork (approx. 30-40 minutes).

6. Transfer mixture into a high powered blender, add salt and pepper, and blend until smooth.

7. Taste and add any additional seasonings you prefer.

8. Add sauce to mushrooms and keep the leftovers for another dish.

9. Enjoy!

SALMON WRAPS WITH CILANTRO CAULIFLOWER RICE

Prep time: 30-45 mins • Cook time: 15 mins • 8 Servings

INGREDIENTS FOR WRAPS

- 1 tsp smoked paprika
- 1 tsp garlic powder
- 1 tsp salt
- ½ tsp ground black pepper
- 1 Tbsp avocado oil
- ¼ cup avocado sauce (see recipe below)

- 2 fresh salmon fish filLets
- 1 head of bib lettuce or iceBurg lettuce cup
- 2-3 cup shredded cabbage
- ¼ cup fresh cilantro leaves, chopped
- 1 lime, juiced
- Salt to taste

CILANTRO-LIME CAULIFLOWER RICE

- 1 head cauliflower, washed, cored, and cut into chunks
- 1 Tbsp coconut oil
- 2 Tbsp lime juice

- 1 tsp sea salt
- ½ tsp ground black pepper
- ¼ cup cilantro, chopped

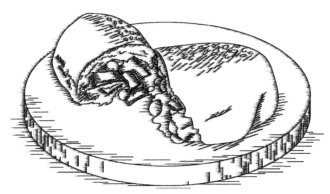

DIRECTIONS FOR AVOCADO SAUCE

- ½ large avocado, peeled, pitted, and quartered
- ¼ cup reduced fat sour cream
- 1 Tbsp plain non-fat Greek yogurt
- 1 tsp lemon juice
- 1 garlic clove, minced

1. Mix all ingredients together until texture is creamy/smooth.

DIRECTIONS FOR WRAPS

1. Season salmon FILLETs generously with paprika, garlic powder, salt, and pepper (or any seasoning of your preference). Lightly pat to adhere, and drizzle with avocado oil.

2. Heat grill to medium high. Grill salmon 5-8 minutes, turning once. Cook just until fillets easily flake but are still moist. Remove from grill and set aside temporarily to cool. NOTE: FILLETs can be pan-fried or baked if you do not have a grill.

3. In a small mixing bowl, combine shredded cabbage with chopped cilantro leaves and juice of 1 lime, salt to taste.

4. Rinse bibb lettuce leaves and lightly blot dry with paper towels. Select the best cup-shaped leaves to create your lettuce wraps.

5. Break apart/shred the cooled salmon FILLETs. Place salmon pieces inside lettuce cups, and sprinkle each with cabbage mixture.

6. Finish each wrap with a drizzle of avocado sauce.

CILANTRO-LIME CAULIFLOWER RICE

1. Place cauliflower in food processor with the grater attachment and pulse until the texture of rice. NOTE: you can also buy pre-made cauliflower rice at the store.

2. Heat skillet on medium heat, add oil. Once hot, add all the ingredients and lightly sauté for approximately 5 minutes, or until it gets to the consistency that you prefer.

3. Remove from heat and add the chopped cilantro and stir until it's evenly distributed.

4. Can either add this into lettuce cup with the salmon and avocado sauce or eat it alongside the wraps.

SAUTÉED CABBAGE

Prep time: 10 mins • Cook time: 20 mins • 8 Servings

INGREDIENTS

- 2 Tbsp extra-virgin olive oil
- 3 lbs green cabbage, cored and finely shredded
- 1 ½ tsp cumin
- 1 ½ TSP salt

DIRECTIONS

1. In a large skillet, heat olive oil over medium heat.

2. Once hot, add shredded cabbage, cumin, and salt. Cook until cabbage is soft, approx. 15-20 minutes (stirring occasionally).

3. Serve as a side with any dish of your choosing!

SEASONED SWEET POTATO FRIES

Prep time: 20 mins • **Cook time: 20 mins** • **4 Servings**

INGREDIENTS FOR FRIES

- 1 large sweet potato
- 2 Tbsp avocado oil
- ½ tsp cumin
- ½ tsp cayenne pepper
- ½ tsp sea salt
- 2 Tbsp nutritional yeast

INGREDIENTS FOR AVOCADO MAYO

- 2 ripe avocados
- ½ cup unsweetened coconut milk
- 3 limes
- ½ tsp sea salt

DIRECTIONS FOR AVOCADO MAYO

1. Cut avocado in half, remove pit, and spoon out the avocado into a blender.

2. Add coconut milk, salt, and lime juice. NOTE: can add cilantro and horseradish (2 Tbsp) if desired.

3. Blend until smooth.

DIRECTIONS FOR FRIES

1. Preheat oven to 425 degrees F.

2. Peel sweet potatoes and cut into "fry" pieces (should get 30-40 fries from 1 large potato).

3. Add the fries into a large bowl.

4. Toss the sweet potato fries in avocado oil.

5. Add seasonings (better to add one at a time and toss after each, add nutritional yeast last).

6. Line baking sheet with parchment paper and arrange sweet potato fries (try to make sure only 1 layer) and cook for 5-10 minutes and then flip and cook for an additional 5-10 minutes.

7. Can serve with avocado mayo (see recipe below) and enjoy!

SHRIMP AND GRITS

Prep time: 10 mins • **Cook time: 30 mins** • **4 Servings**

INGREDIENTS

- 1 lb shrimp, peeled and deveined
- 2 Tbsp ghee butter (divided)
- 2 cloves garlic, minced
- 2 tsp paprika
- ½ tsp onion powder
- ¼ tsp cayenne pepper

- 1 head cauliflower, washed, cored, and cut into chunks
- ½ cup lite coconut milk
- 1 Tbsp nutritional yeast
- Salt and pepper to taste
- Hot sauce (optional)

DIRECTIONS FOR THE GRITS

1. Place cauliflower in a large pot with 1 cup water. Bring to a boil and cover.

2. Boil cauliflower for 20 minutes or until tender when poked with a fork.

3. Once done, drain cauliflower and place in blender. Add milk, 1 Tbsp butter, salt, pepper, and nutritional yeast. Pulse until mixture is a smooth texture.

DIRECTIONS FOR THE SHRIMP

1. Melt 1 Tbsp ghee butter over medium heat. Once melted, add garlic and sauté for 1 minute.

2. Add shrimp, paprika, cayenne pepper, and onion powder and cook for 6 minutes. Stir occasionally.

3. Serve cauliflower grits in bowl and top with shrimp and sauce, can add hot sauce if desired.

4. Enjoy!

SLOW COOKED HEARTY CHILI

Prep time: 15 mins • Cook time: 6-6.5 hours • 8 Servings

INGREDIENTS

- 2 Tbsp extra virgin olive oil (divided)
- 2 lbs grass-fed ground beef
- 4 cloves garlic, minced
- 1 medium onion, finely diced
- 3 stalks celery, finely diced
- 2 Tbsp chili powder
- 2 tsp ground cumin
- ¼ tsp ground cinnamon

- 1 pinch ground cloves
- 2 cups bone broth
- 1 15-ounce can sweet potato puree
- 1 Tbsp adobo sauce from preserved chipotles
- 2 tsp red wine vinegar
- 2 tsp coconut aminos
- Topping options: sour cream, avocado, diced scallions, lime wedge

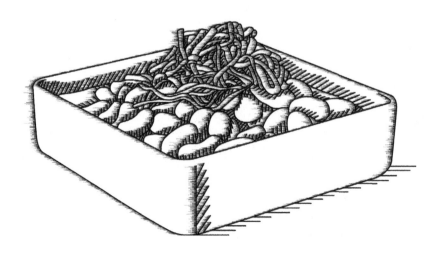

1. Heat 1 Tbsp oil in a large nonstick skillet over high heat.

2. Once hot, add 1 lb ground beef and ½ teaspoon salt, and cook for 3-4 minutes, or until browned. Break the meat apart with a spatula while cooking.

3. Transfer to Instant Pot (or can use a slow cooker) and repeat with the remaining beef.

4. Once done cooking beef, turn heat on stove down to medium and heat the remaining teaspoon oil in the same skillet.

5. Add the garlic, onion, and celery, and cook for 5 minutes, until soft.

6. Add the chili powder, cumin, cinnamon, and stir, cooking for 1 minute.

7. Pour in the broth, stir and scrape the bottom of the pan, then transfer to the Instant Pot.

8. After broth mixture is added to Instant Pot, add sweet potato puree, adobo sauce, wine vinegar, coconut aminos, 2 teaspoons salt, and pepper to taste.

9. Cover pot and set to "Slow Cook" on medium setting for 6 hours. Be sure the knob is turned to vent the steam.

10. Serve with scallions, lime wedges, and sour cream, if desired.

SPICED UP
CHICKEN ENCHILADAS

Prep time: 15 mins • Cook time: 45 mins • 8 Enchiladas

INGREDIENTS

- 2 Tbsp coconut oil
- 8 oz shiitake mushrooms, chopped
- 1 medium yellow onion, chopped
- 12 oz chicken breast (approx. 2 large breasts), boneless, skinless
- 2 cups chicken bone broth, divided
- ½ tsp salt
- ¼ tsp pepper
- 8 oz goat cheese, crumbled
- 4 cloves garlic, peeled
- 3 tsp apple cider vinegar
- 1 tsp coconut aminos
- ½ tsp ground cumin
- ½ tsp dried oregano
- ¼ tsp paprika
- 8 Siete tortillas (grain-free), warmed

DIRECTIONS

1. Preheat oven to 350 degrees F.

2. Start by cooking chicken: in skillet, heat butter over medium heat. Add chicken and cook thoroughly (for approx. 15-20 minutes, flipping halfway). Once done cooking, make sure internal temperature is 165 degree F.

3. While oven is preheating and your chicken is cooking, heat oil in a large nonstick skillet over medium heat.

4. Add the mushrooms and onions and cook until soft (approx. 6-8 minutes). Stir often.

5. Shred the cooked chicken and then add to the mushrooms and onions, along with ½ cup broth, ½ teaspoon salt, and ¼ teaspoon pepper. Reduce heat to medium and cook until most of the liquid is absorbed, approx. 3-4 minutes.

6. Transfer to a large bowl and stir in half the goat cheese (4oz).

7. Make adobo sauce by pulsing the remaining broth, garlic, cider vinegar, coconut aminos, cumin, oregano, and paprika in a blender until very, very smooth, about 3 minutes.

8. Pour ½ cup of the adobo sauce into the bottom of a 9-by-13-inch glass baking dish.

9. Scoop ¼ cup of mushroom mixture into each tortilla, roll the tortilla, and place seam-side down in the pan.

10. Once all the tortillas are placed side-by-side, pour the remaining adobo sauce evenly over the top and sprinkle with the remaining goat cheese.

11. Bake at 350 degrees F for approx. 15 minutes or until the sauce is bubbling and the goat cheese is melted.

12. Serve and enjoy!

SPICY CAULIFLOWER AND CHICKEN

Prep time: 15 mins • Cook time: 35 mins • 6 Servings

INGREDIENTS

- 1.5 lbs chicken (breast cut into bite sized chunks)
- 1 head cauliflower (washed, cored, and cut into chunks)
- 2 Tbsp coconut oil
- 2/3 cup raw honey
- 3 Tbsp Sriracha
- ¼ cup coconut aminos

- 4 cloves garlic, minced
- 2 tsp onion powder
- ½ cup cold water + 2 Tbsp arrowroot flour
- Salt and pepper to taste
- Scallions chopped (optional for garnish)

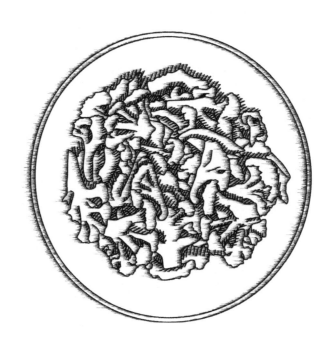

1. Preheat oven to 400 degrees F.

2. Line a baking sheet with parchment paper.

3. Toss cauliflower in 1 Tbsp coconut oil (melted) and sprinkle with a pinch of salt.

4. Place on baking sheet and cook for 25 minutes, then cool for approx. 10 minutes.

5. While cauliflower is cooking, heat a large skillet with 1 Tbsp coconut oil.

6. Once pan is hot, place chicken chunks into pan and cook through (turning every few minutes). This should take anywhere from 7-9 minutes. Once cooked thoroughly, remove pan from heat.

7. Make sauce on stove in a small saucepan: combine garlic, sriracha, coconut aminos, honey, and onion powder.

8. Once sauce mixture is brought to a boil, reduce heat and let simmer. Make sure to stir occasionally.

9. As the sauce simmers, whisk together water and arrowroot flour in a small bowl until it dissolves. Keep whisking this slurry while you add it to the sriracha sauce mixture.

10. Raise heat to bring to a boil again. After brought to a boil, lower heat again and cook until the sauce thickens.

11. Once thickened to your preference, remove from heat and allow it to cool. Keep in mind the sauce will continue to thicken as it cools.

12. In a large bowl, stir together the cooked chicken, roasted cauliflower, and sauce.

13. You can add more salt, pepper, and sriracha if you desire.

14. Garnish with the chopped scallions and enjoy!

SPICY TEMPEH BOWL

Prep time: 15 mins • **Cook time: 10 mins** • **1 Serving**

INGREDIENTS FOR BOWL

- 1 Tbsp coconut oil
- 2 cups spinach
- 4 ounces tempeh, sliced into thin triangles
- 2 Tbsp homemade sauce (see below)

- ½ small yellow onion, diced
- ½ avocado, diced
- 1 cup baked or grilled, cubed/peeled sweet potato

INGREDIENTS/DIRECTIONS FOR SAUCE

- ¼ cup + 2 Tbsp mayonnaise (avocado and oil based)
- 2 ½ tsp sriracha
- 2 1/4 Tbsp ketchup
- 1 ½ tsp coconut aminos
- 1 garlic clove, minced

1. Whisk all sauce ingredients together

1. Warm a skillet over high heat, add the oil.

2. When oil is hot, add the tempeh triangles to one side of the pan and the onion to the other.

3. Sauté for 2 minutes, then flip triangles.

4. After flipping, smother with homemade "bang-bang sauce" and cook for another 1-3 minutes or until the edges begin to blacken. Flip a few more times during this process. Flip the onions a few times as well.

   NOTE: If the tempeh gets too dry in the pan add a teaspoon of water.

5. Sprinkle some fresh black pepper over top the onions and turn off stove and set pan aside.

6. In a serving bowl, add the spinach and top with the saucy tempeh, onions, avocado and sweet potato.

7. If there is any "bang-bang sauce left", feel free to drizzle over top of salad!

SPINACH CAULIFLOWER MASH

Prep time: 10 mins • Cook time: 20 mins • 4 Servings

INGREDIENTS

- 1 large head cauliflower, washed, cored, cut into large chunks
- 2 Tbsp avocado oil
- 1 cup yellow onion, finely diced
- 2 cups spinach
- 1/8 tsp garlic powder
- 2 tbsp ghee butter
- Salt and pepper to taste

1. In a medium pot bring water to boil. Add cauliflower and cook until tender (approx. 10 minutes).

2. While cauliflower is cooking, add oil to skillet and heat. Once oil is hot, add onions and sauté for 4-5 minutes.

3. Add spinach, toss, and then remove from stove.

4. Once cauliflower is done cooking, drain the water (keep 1 cup).

5. Place cauliflower in food processor or blender and pulse until rice consistency.

6. Add spinach, salt, pepper, ghee butter, and garlic powder to cauliflower and pulse until combine, do not over mix (be careful as it can become pureed very quickly).

7. You can add the retained water and add to cauliflower if it is too thick.

8. Serve with any dish or just eat it by itself!

SWEET POTATO QUICHE

Prep time: 20 mins • **Cook time: 1.5 hours** • **10 Servings**

INGREDIENTS

- 2 lbs sweet potato, washed, peeled, grated
- 1 tsp salt
- 1 tsp ground black pepper
- 9 pasteurized eggs
- 2 Tbsp ghee butter
- ¼ cup coconut milk
- 4 oz goat cheese, crumbled

1. Preheat oven to 450 degrees F.

2. Line a 9-inch spring form pan with parchment paper (bottom and sides) or can use a 9-inch pie pan and grease with cooking spray.

3. Use a clean kitchen towel to squeeze any moisture from grated sweet potatoes (place them on towel, gather corners together and squeeze out any moisture).

4. In a medium bowl, whisk 1 egg, ½ tsp pepper, and ½ tsp salt. Add sweet potatoes and mix until combined.

5. Press the sweet potato mixture on the bottom of the pan and then bake for 30 minutes.

6. Once done cooking, remove from oven and reduce oven temperature to 350 degrees F.

7. In a bowl, whisk 8 eggs, pepper, salt, and coconut milk. Once combined, add 2 oz goat cheese and stir.

8. Pour egg mixture into sweet potato crust and sprinkle the remaining goat cheese on top.

9. Bake for 30 minutes or until the center is mostly set.

10. Remove from oven and let sit for approx. 10 minutes before digging in!

BACON AND CHEESE COVERED CHICKEN

Prep time: 5 mins • Cook time: 40 mins • 6 Servings

INGREDIENTS

- 2 ½ - 3 lbs chicken breasts, cut in half width wise
- 2 Tbsp seasoning rub (see recipe below)
- ½ lb bacon, cut strips in half
- 4 oz shredded cheddar

SEASONING RUB INGREDIENTS

- 1 ½ cup garlic powder
- ½ cup dried thyme
- ½ cup dried parsley
- 1/3 cup onion powder
- 4 Tbsp sweet paprika
- 4 Tbsp cayenne pepper

1. Mix together and portion out what you need for this recipe and save the rest for another day!

1. Preheat oven to 400 F.

2. Spray a large baking sheet with cooking spray.

3. Coat all sides of chicken breast with seasoning rub and place on greased baking sheet.

4. Top each piece of chicken with a strip of bacon.

5. Bake for 30 min on the top rack, until the chicken is 165 degrees F and the bacon looks crispy.

6. Remove from the oven and sprinkle the cheese on top of the bacon. Put back in the oven for about 10 minutes or until the cheese is bubbly and golden.

7. Serve with a side of roasted cauliflower and Brussels sprouts and enjoy!

BACON AND CHEESE SLIDER

Prep time: 15 mins • Cook time: 35 mins • 10 Servings

INGREDIENTS

- 1 large sweet potato, washed and sliced into 10 rounds - ¼ - ½ inch thick
- 2 Tbsp extra virgin olive oil
- 5 slices turkey bacon, cut in half to make 10 pieces total
- 1 ½ lbs ground beef (shape them into 10 small patties)
- 1 thick slice onion
- 1 oz buffalo mozzarella cheese
- Salt and pepper, to taste

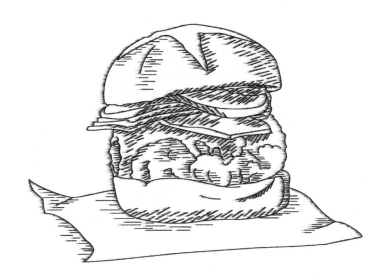

1. Line a large baking sheet with parchment paper and preheat oven to 425 degrees F.

2. Lightly brush each side of the sweet potato rounds with olive oil and place them on the baking sheet, lightly sprinkle with salt.

3. Roast sweet potatoes in the preheated oven for 30-35 minutes. For even cooking, flip once in the middle of roasting. They are done when the outside is lightly browned and the inside is soft.

4. While the sweet potatoes are roasting, place bacon in a large skillet over medium-high heat. Cook until crisp, and then remove them from pan, place strips on paper towels to drain.

5. In the same pan (bottom can still be coated with bacon grease), turn the heat back to medium-high heat.

6. Place the burger patties in pan and cook for approx. 4-5 minutes on each side, or until they are done to your preference.

7. To assemble slider, place roasted sweet potato rounds on a plate. Place burger patties on top of rounds. Layer with a strip of bacon, a slice of cheese, and an onion slice.

8. Add a dollop of avocado mayo or Baja cream sauce and pair with spicy jicama fries.

9. Enjoy!

CAESAR SALAD WITH BLACKENED SHRIMP

Prep time: 15 mins • Cook time: 10 mins • 2 Servings

INGREDIENTS

For the Salad

- ½ lb shrimp, peeled and deveined
- 2 Tbsp blackened seasoning (see recipe below)
- 1 Tbsp extra virgin olive oil
- Juice of lemon
- 1 head romaine, leaves washed and torn
- Shaved Parmesan cheese, for garnish
- Diced red onion and cucumber (optional topping)

For the Seasoning

- 2 ½ Tbsp paprika
- 1 Tbsp sea salt
- 1 Tbsp smoked salt
- 2 Tbsp garlic powder
- 1 Tbsp black pepper
- 1 Tbsp onion powder
- 1 Tbsp cayenne pepper
- 1 Tbsp dried oregano

For the Dressing (1 cup)

- 1 egg yolk, room temperature
- 1 cup extra virgin olive oil
- 1-2 cloves garlic, crushed
- 4 Tbsp fresh lemon juice
- 1 ½ tsp anchovy paste
- 1 ½ tsp Dijon mustard
- ½ tsp ground black pepper

DIRECTIONS

1. To make the dressing: add all of your dressing ingredients to a large mason jar (or other medium sized container).

2. Use an immersion blender to blend ingredients until the dressing has emulsified.

3. After a few seconds, stir and taste. Add additional seasoning as desired.

4. NOTE: if you don't have an immersion blender, you can make this in a high powered blender - just toss all of your ingredients in and blend for about 30 seconds or until it emulsifies. Chill until ready to use.

5. To prepare the shrimp: place shrimp in a bowl and toss with lemon juice and 2 Tbsp blackened seasoning.

6. Heat oil in a non-stick skillet over medium-high heat. Once hot, add shrimp and cook 2-3 minutes per side.

7. Assemble salad: place romaine lettuce in a large mixing bowl, drizzle the dressing on top and mix well until the leaves are coated (start with a small amount of dressing and add as you go until the leaves are covered to your preference). Place mixture on top of two plates and top with the blackened shrimp and shaved Parmesan.

8. Can also top salad with diced red onion and cucumbers!

CHEESE DIP
FOR VEGGIES

Prep time: 5 mins • Cook time: 2 hours • 6-8 Servings

INGREDIENTS

- 1 (15-ounce) can chili (no beans)
- 1 lb ground beef, cooked and drained
- 10 oz cheddar cheese
- 4 oz cream cheese, softened
- 1 can roasted red peppers, not drained
- Juice of a lemon
- 1 (4-ounce) can green chilies, diced

Toppings:
- jalapeños, diced
- Avocado, diced
- Sour cream

1. Turn slow cooker on low and add chili, beef, cheddar cheese, cream cheese, and chilies.

2. Cook until creamy (approx. 2 hours).

3. Top with jalapeños, avocado, and sour cream.

4. Serve and enjoy!

CHICKEN AND ARTICHOKE PASTA

Prep time: 10 mins • **Cook time: 10 mins** • **4 Servings**

INGREDIENTS

For the Salad

- 1 cup tapioca flour PLUS extra for dusting
- 1 cup almond flour, super fine (DO NOT use almond meal)
- 1 tsp salt
- 2 large eggs
- 1-2 Tbsp extra virgin olive oil
- 1 (14oz) can artichoke hearts, chopped
- 1 lb boneless, skinless chicken breast chopped into bite size pieces

For the Sauce

- ¾ cup coconut milk
- 2 Tbsp lemon juice, freshly squeezed
- 2 Tbsp nutritional yeast
- 2 cloves garlic, minced
- 1 Tbsp extra virgin olive oil
- Salt and pepper to taste
- Red pepper flakes, optional

To prepare the Sauce

1. Add all ingredients for the sauce to a high powered blender and blend until it's creamy and smooth.

2. Taste and adjust the seasonings as needed.

3. Set aside/refrigerate until ready to use.

1. Mix together tapioca flour, almond flour and salt in a medium bowl.

2. Make a small hole in the middle of the flour mixture and crack in the eggs. Stir eggs with fork, and work your way out, incorporating more and more of the flour.

3. Once the egg is mostly incorporated, use your hands and knead the mixture, making sure to add a bit more tapioca flour if the dough sticks to your fingers.

4. Once thoroughly combined/kneaded, divide dough into 3 portions.

5. Dust a cutting board and rolling pin with tapioca flour.

6. Take one of the portions of dough and lightly dust with tapioca flour as well. Roll the dough to approx. 1/8 inch thickness. Use a pizza cutter to cut into desired thickness of noodles.

7. In a large pot, boil 4 quarts of water and drizzle in approx. 1-2 Tbsp of olive oil.

8. Once water is boiling, add noodles and cook for 2 minutes.

9. Remove from water with a slotted spoon and place in strainer. Drizzle with olive oil to keep noodles from sticking. Repeat process until all dough has been cooked.

10. At the same time you are cooking noodles (or after noodles are done), begin to prepare the chicken: heat 1-2 Tbsp ghee butter in a large skillet over medium-high heat. Once butter is somewhat melted, add chopped chicken and sauté until chicken is no longer pink.

11. Add artichoke hearts to skillet and cook for approx. 3-4 minutes.

12. You can add the noodles and sauce to skillet and mix together, heating everything thoroughly.

13. Portion servings into a bowl or on a plate and top with chopped parsley and shaved Parmesan if you desire. Enjoy!

CHICKEN FRIED STEAK

Prep time: 1 hour • Cook time: 30 mins • 4 Servings

INGREDIENTS

For the Steak

- 2-3 lbs top round or top sirloin steak, tenderize with a spiked mallet
- 2 eggs
- 1 Tbsp brown mustard
- salt and pepper, to taste
- 1 7 oz bag of plantain chips
- ½ cup tapioca flour
- 1 tsp garlic powder
- ¼ tsp dried thyme
- ¼ tsp parsley
- ¼ tsp cayenne
- 4 Tbsp coconut oil

For the Gravy

- 2 Tbsp ghee butter
- 12 oz pork breakfast sausage
- ½ cup mushrooms, sliced
- 2/3 cup onion, diced
- 3 cloves garlic, minced
- 1 ½ cups heavy cream
- 1 tbsp fresh parsley, chopped
- Salt and pepper, to taste

DIRECTIONS

1. In a small bowl, whisk eggs and mustard together. Pour mixture into a large dish.

2. Place the steaks in the egg mixture, making sure to turn in order to coat evenly. Cover the dish and refrigerate for an hour.

3. While the steaks are marinating, make the gravy: heat butter in a large skillet over medium-high heat. Add sausage and mushrooms, cook until browned, breaking apart sausage with a wooden spoon. Once sausage is done cooking, remove and set aside. Reduce heat to low and add onion and garlic to pan and cook until onions are translucent - make sure to stir so it doesn't burn. Add cream, salt, and pepper and let simmer, sauce should thicken. You can add tapioca starch to help thicken it. Once gravy is at your desired consistency, add the sausage and mushrooms to it and warm through.

4. While the gravy cooks, place the plantain chips in a food processor and grind them until they look like coarse sand.

5. Add the garlic powder, tapioca flour, thyme, parsley, and cayenne to the ground plantains and stir to combine. Place this mixture in a large shallow dish.

6. Remove the steaks from the refrigerator.

7. Heat 4 Tbsp coconut oil in a large skillet over medium heat.

8. Remove the steaks from the egg mixture and let the excess drip off for a second.

9. Place the steaks in the ground plantains, coat each side evenly. Shake off any excess breading.

10. Carefully place the breaded steaks into the hot skillet and cook 4-5 minutes. Remove steaks and place on a wire rack. This step will need to be done in batches, so repeat with remaining steaks.

11. Serve steaks and pour sausage and mushroom gravy on top. Garnish with chopped parsley.

12. Enjoy!

CHEESY CHICKEN PARMESAN

Prep time: 15 mins • Cook time: 15-20 mins • 4 Servings

INGREDIENTS FOR CHICKEN PARMESAN

- 4 boneless, skinless chicken breasts
- 2 Tbsp ghee butter
- 2 cloves garlic, crushed
- 6 oz homemade marinara sauce (see recipe below)
- cup parmesan cheese, grated
- Fresh basil, chopped
- Salt and pepper, to taste

INGREDIENTS FOR MARINARA SAUCE

- 1 Tbsp coconut oil
- 1 yellow onion, chopped
- 2 garlic cloves, minced
- ½ lb carrots, chopped
- 1 medium beet, chopped
- 1 cup water
- 1 tsp salt
- Pepper to taste

DIRECTIONS FOR CHICKEN PARMESAN

1. Preheat broiler.

2. Heat butter in large skillet over medium heat.

3. Add garlic and cook for 1 minute.

4. Lightly salt and pepper chicken and then place breasts into skillet. Cook until chicken is browned.

5. When browned, place chicken on nonstick baking sheet (or line sheet with foil).

6. Top each with about 1 tablespoon pasta sauce and parmesan cheese.

7. Place baking sheet under broiler and broil chicken for about 4 minutes or until cheese is melted.

DIRECTIONS FOR MARINARA SAUCE

1. Place a large pot on the stove and turn heat to medium, add coconut oil.

2. Once coconut oil melted, add onions and sauté until tender and lightly golden.

3. Add minced garlic and sauté for 1-2 minutes.

4. Add carrots, water, and beets and bring to a boil.

5. Cover and lower heat to a simmer, cooking until beets and carrots are tender when poked with a fork (approx. 30-40 minutes).

6. Transfer mixture into a high powered blender, add salt and pepper, and blend until smooth.

7. Taste and add any additional seasonings you prefer.

8. Add sauce to mushrooms and keep the leftovers for another dish.

9. Enjoy!

CREAMY MUSHROOM STUFFED CHICKEN

Prep time: 10 mins • Cook time: 30 mins • 4 Servings

INGREDIENTS

Garlic Parmesan Cream Sauce

- 1 Tbsp extra virgin olive oil
- 2 large cloves garlic, minced
- 1 Tbsp Dijon mustard
- ¾ cup full fat milk
- ¾ cup reduced fat cream
- ½ cup Parmesan cheese, grated
- Salt and pepper, to taste
- ½ tsp tapioca flour (for thickening, may need a little more if you want a thicker sauce)
- 2 Tbsp fresh parsley, chopped

Chicken

- 4 boneless, skinless chicken breast
- 1 tsp onion powder
- 1 tsp dried parsley
- 2 cups crumbled goat cheese
- ¼ cup parmesan cheese, grated
- Salt and pepper, to taste

Mushrooms

- 4 Tbsp extra virgin olive oil
- 8 oz Portobello mushrooms, sliced
- 4 cloves garlic, minced
- Salt and pepper, to taste

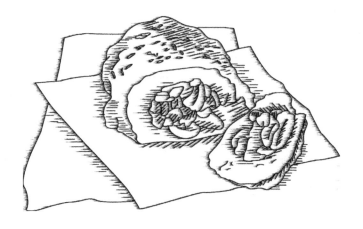

1. Preheat oven to 400°F.

2. Heat 4 Tbsp olive oil in a large skillet over medium heat. Add garlic and sauté until fragrant (about 1 minute). Add in mushrooms, salt and pepper (to taste). Cook until soft, stirring occasionally. Set aside and allow to cool while preparing your chicken.

3. In a small bowl, mix together salt, pepper, onion powder and dried parsley. Coat each piece of chicken (all sides) evenly with seasoning mixture.

4. Horizontally slice a slit through the thickest part of each breast to form a pocket. Place crumbled goat cheese into the pocket you created. Make sure to evenly distribute the goat cheese between each piece of chicken.

5. Take the mushroom mixture and divide evenly into 4 servings, place inside pocket of chicken (leave the juices from the mushroom mixture in the pan).

6. Top the mushroom mixture with 1 tablespoon of parmesan cheese per breast.

7. Poke two or three toothpicks into the chicken to keep the mushrooms inside while cooking.

8. Heat the same pan the mushrooms were in along with the pan juices. Add the chicken and sear until golden, flipping to make sure each side slightly browns. Cover pan and place in preheated oven, cook for 20 minutes or until cooked through and no longer pink (internal temp of chicken should be 165 degrees F).

9. While chicken is cooking, you can prepare the cream sauce: you can either use the same pan you have been using, or heat a clean pan with 1 Tbsp olive oil. Add garlic and cook until fragrant, approx. 1 minute. Reduce heat to low heat, and add the mustard, milk, and cream.

10. Bring the sauce to a gentle simmer and add in any remaining mushrooms and parmesan cheese. Let the sauce simmer until the parmesan cheese has slightly melted. Gradually mix in tapioca flour to thicken. Season with a little salt and pepper to taste.

11. Once the chicken is done baking, add to the pan with sauce. Take a spoon and scoop the sauce from the pan and drizzle over the chicken, repeat multiple times.

12. Add chicken on top of Miracle Noodles with additional sauce and parsley on top!

CRISPY CARAMELIZED ONION AND GOAT CHEESE PIZZA

Prep time: 20 mins • Cook time: 40-45 mins • Makes two 10" pizzas

INGREDIENTS

- 1 ½ cups tapioca flour
- 1 cup arrowroot flour
- 2 tsp sea salt
- 1 tsp onion powder
- 1 tsp garlic powder
- 2 eggs
- ½ cup extra virgin olive oil, plus more for oiling dough
- 1 cup water
- 1 medium white onion, cut into thin rings
- Salt and pepper
- 1-2 Tbsp olive oil for sautéing
- 3 oz goat cheese
- Splash milk
- Fresh arugula for topping

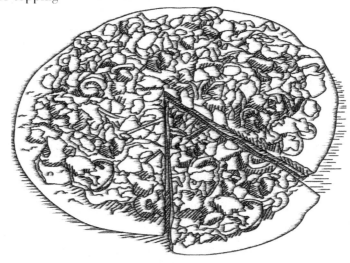

1. Preheat your oven to 425 degrees F and place two baking sheets/pizza stones inside oven.

2. In a medium mixing bowl, combine tapioca and arrowroot flour, salt, onion powder, and garlic powder. Mix to combine.

3. Add eggs, olive oil, and water, mix well.

4. Set dough aside for about 5 minutes to allow it to firm up a little.

5. In a medium skillet, sauté onion in 1-2 Tbsp olive oil over medium heat, stirring frequently. Season with salt and pepper. Continue to cook onions until begin browning (approx. 15 minutes). Set aside once cooked.

6. To prepare dough, coat your hands in olive oil or spray with cooking spray, then scoop up the dough and divide it in half. Form one half into a ball. Place it on parchment paper and press it into the form of a 10 inch crust with your hands. Do the same with the second half.

7. Slide the dough and parchment paper onto pizza stone (or baking sheet) and bake for approx. 11-14 minutes.

8. While the crust is baking, spoon goat cheese into a bowl and add a splash of milk or water to thin it so it's spreadable. Whisk until smooth.

9. Remove pizza crust from oven and spread the goat cheese and onions evenly on top.

10. Place back in the oven and bake for an additional 5-10 minutes, or until the edges appear crisp and the onions and goat cheese have warmed through.

11. Remove from oven and drizzle with additional olive oil or a balsamic glaze and top with fresh arugula. Slice and enjoy!

CRISPY CHICKEN TENDERS WITH CREAMY SRIRACHA SAUCE

Prep time: 5 mins • **Cook time: 15 mins** • **7 Tenders**

INGREDIENTS

- 1 ½ lb chicken
- 1/3 cup coconut flour
- 1 cup almond flour
- 2 large eggs
- 1 Tbsp coconut milk
- ½ tsp salt
- ¼ tsp ground black pepper
- ½ tsp garlic powder
- ½ tsp onion powder

For the Dipping Sauce

- 1 cup paleo mayo
- 1 tsp garlic powder
- ¼ tsp paprika
- 4 Tbsp sriracha

DIRECTIONS

1. Preheat oven to 425° and line a baking sheet with parchment paper. Set aside.

2. You will need to bread the chicken in 3 different steps, so you will need 3 shallow, flat-bottomed dishes.

3. Put the coconut flour in the first bowl.

4. Whisk the eggs and coconut milk together in the second bowl.

5. Mix together the almond flour, salt, pepper, garlic, and onion in the third bowl.

6. Taking one strip at a time, dip in the coconut flour (making sure it is fully coated), then dip it in the egg mixture and let any extra drip off. Lastly, dip it in the almond flour mixture and make sure it's fully coated with no wet spots showing.

7. Once you have dipped the chicken strip in each bowl as described, place it on the lined baking sheet and repeat with remaining tenders.

8. NOTE: to help tenders brown, spray them with olive oil or coconut oil.

9. Bake for 10 minutes, then flip them over and bake for 5 additional minutes.

10. If you want them to be extra brown/crispy, turn the oven to 500 degrees F and bake for 5 additional minutes.

11. While the tenders are baking, mix together all the ingredients for the dipping sauce.

12. Serve and enjoy!

CURRY SHRIMP WITH CAULIFLOWER RICE

Prep time: 10 mins • **Cook time: 15 mins** • **2 Servings**

INGREDIENTS

- 3 cloves garlic, minced (approx. 1 ½ Tbsp)
- ½ Tbsp ginger, minced
- 1 cup yellow onion, diced
- 1 Tbsp coconut oil
- ½ lb shrimp, peeled and deveined (can use chicken as well)
- 2 Tbsp green curry paste
- 1 cup broccoli florets
- 1 can full-fat coconut milk
- 1 Tbsp scallions, finely sliced
- 2 cups cilantro-lime cauliflower rice
- Salt and ground pepper to taste

1. Heat oil in pan over medium high heat.

2. Once oil is hot, add garlic, ginger and onion. Stir until fragrant and translucent, approx. 3 minutes.

3. Add shrimp, with a small pinch of salt, and cook for 30 seconds.

4. Add broccoli and coconut milk. Stir and bring to a gentle simmer.

5. Add in green curry paste and stir until well incorporated.

6. Bring mixture to a gentle simmer again and cook until sauce is thickened, approx. 6-7 minutes.

   NOTE: if you want the sauce to be a bit thicker, you can gradually add tapioca flour.

7. Taste and add salt or additional green curry paste if desired.

8. Top with scallions and serve over hot cilantro-lime cauliflower rice.

DECONSTRUCTED DEVILED EGG PASTA SALAD

Prep time: 20 mins • **Cook time: 30-40 mins** • **8 Servings**

INGREDIENTS

- 1 (16oz) box of gluten-free rotini noodles
- 1½ cups paleo mayo
- 3 Tbsp sour cream
- 2 Tbsp mustard
- 2 Tbsp sweet pickle relish
- 6 hard boiled eggs, sliced
- ¼ cup red bell pepper, diced
- ¼ cup onion, diced
- 2-3 stalks celery, finely chopped
- 3 Tbsp fresh dill, chopped
- 1 tsp paprika
- salt and pepper to taste

DIRECTIONS

1. Prepare pasta according to package instructions, drain, and let cool completely.

2. Make hard boiled eggs as you usually do. Once done, peel and slice.

3. Place noodles in a large bowl and add all ingredients, except the eggs. Mix well.

4. Add eggs and gently fold them into mix.

5. Place mixture in refrigerator until ready to serve.

6. Top with diced scallions and sliced olives, enjoy!

DECONSTRUCTED
FISH TACOS

Prep time: 20 mins • **Cook time: 10 mins** • **6 Servings**

(Fish should marinate for 2-6 hours)

INGREDIENTS

For the Baja Cream Sauce

- ½ cup paleo mayo
- ¾ cup sour cream
- 3 Tbsp lime juice
- 1 tsp garlic powder
- 2 tsp sriracha sauce
- 1 tsp salt
- ½ tsp pepper
- ½ tsp cumin
- ½ tsp cayenne
- 1 tsp honey

For the Fish

- 1 ½ - 2 lbs cod (or other firm white fish)
- 3 limes freshly squeezed (enough for 1/3 cup)
- ½ - 1 tsp chipotle powder
- ½ tsp sea salt
- 1-2 Tbsp extra virgin olive oil (for cooking fish in skillet)

For the Bowls

- 1 small head of cabbage, shredded
- 1 ripe avocado, diced
- Diced red onion (optional for topping)

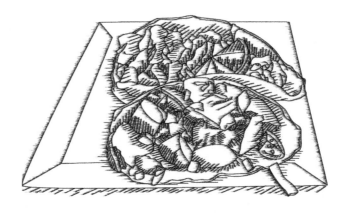

DIRECTIONS

1. Place the fish in a large shallow dish or ziptop bag.

2. Combine the lime juice, dried chipotle powder, and sea salt. Pour it over the fish.

3. Place fish in fridge to let it chill and marinate for at least 2 hours (up to 6 hours).

4. Combine all of the ingredients for the Baja cream sauce and chill until ready to serve.

5. Two options for cooking the fish: grill it over medium-high heat in a greased grill pan OR in a skillet.

6. If cooking in a skillet, then heat olive oil over medium-high heat and lay fish into pan. Cook each side until brown (approx. 2-3 minutes per side).

7. When ready to assemble your bowls: place a bed of shredded cabbage in each bowl and lay the fish on top, drizzle with Baja cream sauce, and top with diced avocado and onion.

8. You can also serve this with cilantro-lime cauliflower rice!

FIESTA RAVIOLI

Prep time: 20 mins • **Cook time: 40 mins** • **8 Servings**

INGREDIENTS

- 1 package gluten-free cheese-filled ravioli
- 1 container (7.5 oz) chive & onion cream cheese spread
- 3 cups shredded rotisserie chicken (cooked from deli) SAVE $
- 1 can (4.5 oz) green chiles, chopped
- 2 cups shredded Mexican cheese blend (8 oz)
- 1 can (10 oz) enchilada sauce
- Sour cream
- Avocado, diced

DIRECTIONS

1. Preheat oven to 375°F.

2. Spray 13x9-inch (3-quart) baking dish with cooking spray (or grease with butter).

3. Cook ravioli as directed on package; drain.

4. Place cream cheese spread in a microwave safe bowl, uncovered, on high for approx. 20 seconds or until soft. Add chicken and chilies, mix well.

5. Spread mixture evenly in the greased baking dish. Sprinkle chicken layer with 1 cup of cheese.

6. Add the cooked ravioli.

7. Pour enchilada sauce over ravioli.

8. Cover dish with foil.

9. Bake until casserole is bubbly, approx. 25-30 minutes.

10. Sprinkle with remaining 1 cup cheese and bake, uncovered, for an additional 4-5 minutes, or until cheese is melted.

11. Dish onto plate and top with diced avocado and a dollop of sour cream.

HEARTY CHICKEN AND DUMPLINGS

Prep time: 15 mins • **Cook time: 1 hour 20 mins** • **6 Servings**

INGREDIENTS

- 1 whole chicken
- 32oz bone broth (may need more)
- 1 onion, finely chopped
- 2 Tbsp extra virgin olive oil
- 5 large carrots, peeled and sliced
- 3 stalks of celery, sliced
- 1 medium onion, chopped
- ½ tsp garlic powder
- Salt and pepper to taste

For the Dumplings

- 2 ¼ cups all purpose gluten free flour blend
- ¼ tsp xanthan gum
- 2 eggs, beaten
- 1 cup chicken bone broth
- 2 tsp baking powder
- 1 Tbsp parsley, chopped fine
- ½ tsp salt

1. Put the whole chicken in a large sauce pan and cover with broth (will need approx. 6-8 cups of broth to cover the chicken).

2. Bring the pot to a boil and then reduce heat to simmer, covered approx. 1 hour. Skim off the foam at the top as it cooks.

3. When the chicken is almost done simmering, heat oil in a large skillet over medium-high heat. Add the onion, carrots and celery and sauté for approx. 5 minutes.

4. When the chicken is done, remove and let cool.

5. Pour the broth from the chicken to the pan with the vegetables and let it simmer on a medium heat for a few minutes.

6. When the chicken has cooled enough to handle, removed the skin, and tear the meat off the bones and add it to the soup.

7. Season with salt, pepper, and garlic powder.

8. Make the dumplings: combine flour, xanthan gum, baking powder, and salt in a mixing bowl.

9. Then add in the beaten eggs and 1 cup chicken bone broth, mix well. Dumpling dough should be sticky and thick.

10. Drop even sized spoonfuls of it into the soup.

11. Cover and continue to let simmer for 20 minutes.

12. Taste the soup and add additional seasoning per your preference.

13. Serve hot!

HOTTER POCKETS

Prep time: 10 mins • **Cook time: 25 minsw** • **8 Pockets**

INGREDIENTS

- 1 cup almond flour, fine
- 1 cup coconut flour
- 1 cup arrowroot
- 2 tsp baking powder
- 1 tsp salt
- 3 eggs
- 1/3 cup coconut milk
- 3 cups of filling: prosciutto, sliced olives, parmesan cheese

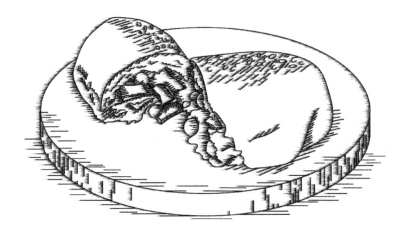

1. Preheat oven to 350 degrees F.

2. Line a baking sheet with aluminum foil and set aside.

3. In a medium bowl, mix together the coconut flour, almond flour baking powder, and salt.

4. In a second bowl, mix together the eggs and milk.

5. Add your bowl of dry ingredients to the bowl with the wet ingredients, mix until combined.

6. Divide dough into 8 portions, roll dough slightly and place prosciutto, olives, and cheese on one side of dough. Fold the other half of the dough over top of the fillers. Brush oil on the top of dough.

7. Roll the edges inward to seal.

8. Bake in the oven for 20 minutes, or until slightly golden brown.

9. Remove from oven and cool slightly before enjoying!

JUICY VEGGIE BURGER

Prep time: 25 mins • **Cook time: 10 mins** • **4 Servings**

INGREDIENTS

- 2 cups walnuts, halves and pieces
- 2 cups mushrooms, chopped
- 1 cup red beet, chopped
- ¼ tsp garlic powder
- ½ cup red onion, chopped
- 1 tsp paprika
- ½ tsp chili powder
- 1 Tbsp parsley, dried
- Dash of salt and ground black pepper
- 2 Tbsp tapioca flour (arrowroot can also be used)
- 3 Tbsp extra-virgin olive oil
- Large butter lettuce leaves or gluten-free bread
- 1 ripe avocado, peeled, pit removed, and sliced
- Buffalo mozzarella cheese or goat cheese

1. You will need a food processor fitted with an S-blade.

2. Add the walnuts, mushrooms, beet, garlic, ¼ cup chopped onions, paprika, chili powder, dried parsley, a dash of salt and pepper to the food processor and pulse until blended, but still chunky.

3. Transfer this mixture to a mixing bowl and stir in the remaining ¼ cup onion and the tapioca flour.

4. Grease your hands with olive oil and knead the mixture to fully combine all of the ingredients.

5. On a sheet of wax paper, form the mixture into four patties, each about 4 inches in diameter and 1 inch thick.

6. Heat 3 Tbsp olive oil in a large skillet over medium-high heat. Add the patties and cook 4 - 5 minutes per side, or until browned.

7. Once done cooking, place each patty on a lettuce leaf .

8. Top with sliced avocado and mozzarella or goat cheese.

9. Drizzle with a balsamic glaze, avocado mayo, or baja cream sauce.

10. Enjoy!

MONGOLIAN BEEF

Prep time: 5 mins • **Cook time: 12-15 mins** • **4 Servings**

INGREDIENTS

- 1 lb beef, sliced at least 1/4" thin
- ¼ tsp salt
- ½ tsp black pepper
- 2 Tbsp arrowroot
- 1 Tbsp extra virgin olive oil
- ¼ cup Stevia brown sugar
- ¼ cup coconut aminos
- 2 garlic cloves minced
- 2 tbsp sweet chili sauce, optional
- ¼ tsp ground ginger
- Scallions, chopped (for garnish)

DIRECTIONS

1. Sauce mixture: in a small bowl, combine the minced garlic, sweet chili sauce, ginger, arrowroot, Stevia brown sugar, salt, and pepper. Set aside.

2. Heat oil in a large pan over medium heat. Add half of the beef to pan and cook 2 minutes per side. Remove onto a plate, repeat with the other half of the beef. Feel free to add more oil to the pan if needed.

3. When the second batch is done, combine all the cooked beef into the pan and pour the sauce over it.

4. Serve with roasted or steamed mixed vegetables and cauliflower mash.

5. Garnish with chopped green onions and enjoy!

NO MAYO
EGG SALAD

Prep time: 10 mins • Cook time: 20 mins • 2-4 Servings

INGREDIENTS

- 6 hard boiled eggs
- 1 ½ avocados (ripe), peeled and roughly mashed
- ¼ cup red onion, diced
- ½ tsp salt (to taste)
- ½ tsp black pepper (to taste)
- ½ Tbsp lemon juice
- 2-4 radishes, washed and sliced
- 2-4 pieces cauliflower toast (homemade) or gluten-free bread

1. Pour several cups of water into a medium pot and add the eggs, making sure that they are completely covered in water.

2. Bring water to a boil and cook for 1 minute, then reduce heat to allow for a simmer. Cover and cook for 15-16 minutes.

3. Once done cooking, drain the water and immediately run cold water over the eggs. Transfer eggs to an ice bath and allow eggs to chill for 10 minutes.

4. Peel shell off of eggs, rinsing any shell pieces left on the eggs. Chop eggs and set aside.

5. Add the avocado to a mixing bowl with the lemon juice, diced onions, salt and pepper. Mash the avocado, leaving it slightly chunky if desired. Add the chopped hard boiled eggs and stir well to combine.

6. Portion out egg salad onto gluten-free bread or homemade cauliflower toast. Top with sliced radishes and enjoy!

SEASONED SWEET POTATO AND CAULIFLOWER

Prep time: 10-15 mins • **Cook time: 25-30 mins** • **3 Servings**

INGREDIENTS FOR RECIPE

- 1-2 Tbsp extra virgin olive oil
- 1 medium head cauliflower, washed, cored, and cut into florets
- 1 onion, finely chopped
- 1 Tbsp fresh ginger, grated
- 1 – 1 ½ Tbsp homemade garam masala (see recipe below)
- 2 tsp chili powder
- 1 large sweet potato, peeled and diced
- Can add additional salt, pepper, and cumin to taste

GARAM MASALA SEASONING RECIPE

- 1 Tbsp ground cumin
- 1 ½ tsp ground coriander
- 1 ½ tsp ground cardamom
- 1 ½ tsp ground black pepper
- 1 tsp ground cinnamon
- ½ tsp ground cloves
- ½ tsp ground nutmeg

1. Mix all ingredients into bowl until well combined. Use the portion you need for this recipe and save the rest for another day!

1. Preheat the oven to 425°F.

2. Lightly grease a baking sheet with oil and place the cauliflower on sheet in a single layer. Drizzle more oil on top of cauliflower, tossing it around to coat the pieces. Roast for 10-15 minutes or until tender and golden on the bottoms and edges.

3. While cauliflower is cooking, heat 1-2 Tbsp oil in a large skillet. Once oil is hot, add the onion and cook for a few minutes, until onions soften.

4. Add the ginger, garam masala, chili powder and any additional cumin, salt, and pepper per your preference. Cook for 1 minute.

5. Add the sweet potatoes and stir to combine thoroughly.

6. Pour ½ cup water over top of mixture and cover with a lid.

7. Reduce the heat to medium-low and cook until the sweet potatoes are tender, approx. 7 minutes.

8. Add the roasted cauliflower to the pan and stir to combine.

9. Serve as a side dish and enjoy!

SHRIMP ALFREDO

Prep time: 10 mins • **Cook time: 15 mins** • **2 Servings**

INGREDIENTS FOR PASTA

- ½ lb shrimp, peeled and deveined
- 2 Tbsp blackened seasoning
- 2 Tbsp extra virgin olive oil
- 2 cloves garlic, minced
- 1 cup cream
- 1/3 -1/2 cup parmesan cheese, grated
- 12 oz Miracle Noodles
- Salt and pepper, to taste

INGREDIENTS/DIRECTIONS SEASONING

- 2 ½ Tbsp paprika
- 1 Tbsp sea salt
- 1 Tbsp smoked salt
- 2 Tbsp garlic powder
- 1 Tbsp black pepper
- 1 Tbsp onion powder
- 1 Tbsp cayenne pepper
- 1 Tbsp dried oregano

1. Mix all ingredients together and use the portion you need for recipe and save the rest for later.

1. Coat shrimp with the blackened seasoning.

2. Heat cast iron pan over medium-high heat and add 1 Tbsp olive oil. Once hot, place seasoned shrimp in a single layer in pan.

3. Cook for 3-4 minutes. Carefully turn shrimp with tongs and cook for another 3-4 minutes, or until shrimp is cooked through and spice is nicely crusted. Set aside.

4. Cook Miracle Noodles as directed on package. Set aside.

5. In a different pan, heat 1 Tbsp oil over medium-high heat. Add garlic and cook until fragrant (approx. 1 min), make sure to lightly stir so it does not burn.

6. Add in cream and parmesan. Stir slowly until heated through and the mixture starts to thicken. Taste and add salt and pepper if needed.

7. Add in cooked noodles and stir until well coated.

8. Serve noodles topped with blackened shrimp and additional grated Parmesan. Enjoy!

SLOPPY JOES

Prep time: 10 mins • Cook time: 10 mins • 6 Servings

INGREDIENTS FOR JOES

- 1 tsp tapioca starch
- ½ cup bone broth
- 2 tsp extra virgin olive oil
- 1 onion, diced
- 1 green bell pepper, diced
- 1 lb ground beef
- 2 Tbsp ketchup

- 2 Tbsp coconut aminos
- 2 tsp taco seasoning
- ¼ tsp salt
- ¼ tsp black pepper
- 1 ½ cups shredded cheese
- 6 homemade gluten free hamburger buns (see recipe below)

INGREDIENTS FOR GLUTEN FREE HAMBURGER BUNS

- 3 cups gluten-free flour blend
- 1 ½ cups coconut milk
- 2 ¼ Tbsp (1 packet) dry active yeast
- 2 Tbsp unsalted butter, melted

- 1 Tbsp apple cider vinegar
- 1 egg + 1 egg white, beaten
- pinch of salt

GLUTEN FREE HAMBURGER BUNS RECIPE

1. Preheat oven to 350 degrees F.

2. In a small saucepan, heat milk over very low heat. Add the packet of yeast, mix until dissolved and let it sit for about 5 minutes.

3. Place remaining ingredients into a medium bowl and mix to combine. Add the milk/yeast mixture. Mix on medium speed for about two minutes, until the dough is smooth.

4. Place the ball of dough on a lightly greased baking sheet. Cover with a warm, damp towel and let sit on the countertop for about an hour.

5. Once done rising, form the dough into palm sized-balls and place on greased baking sheet.

6. Flatten lightly with the palm of your hand.

7. Brush melted butter on top of dough balls and sprinkle with salt.

8. Bake in oven for approx. 50 minutes, until cooked through and golden brown.

DIRECTIONS FOR JOES

1. Preheat broiler.

2. In a small bowl, whisk together broth and tapioca starch. Set aside.

3. Heat oil in a large nonstick skillet over medium high. Add the onion and bell peppers and sauté for approx. 3 minutes, or until tender.

4. Add in the beef and continue to cook for another 3 minutes, breaking it up as it browns. Drain off fat.

5. Stir in the ketchup, coconut aminos, taco seasoning, salt, and pepper.

6. Stir the broth and tapioca starch and it to the skillet; simmer for about 3 minutes, stirring occasionally, until mixture thickens slightly.

7. Scoop desired amount of sloppy Joe mixture onto buns, top with 1/4 cup cheese, and stick under the broiler to allow cheese to melt. (watch closely to ensure nothing burns!)

8. Serve with jicama fries or sweet potato chips and enjoy!

SPICED CAULIFLOWER AND PUMPKIN SOUP

Prep time: 5 mins • Cook time: 10 mins • 4 Cups

INGREDIENTS

- 4 cups cauliflower rice
- ½ cup red onion, diced
- 1 clove garlic, crushed
- 2 Tbsp avocado oil
- 2 tsp pumpkin spice
- 1 can (13.5 ounce) coconut milk, full fat
- 1/8- ¼ tsp allspice (optional)
- Salt and black pepper to taste

1. Heat olive oil in a large skillet over medium heat. Once hot, add onions, garlic, salt, pepper, and allspice, sauté for 2-3 minutes or until the onions are soft.

2. Add the cauliflower rice, entire can of coconut milk, and the pumpkin spice to the skillet and stir until well combined and let simmer until cauliflower rice is soft. Add additional seasonings to your preference.

3. Portion out soup into bowls. Serve with homemade biscuits (see recipe for almond flour biscuits).

4. Enjoy!

SPICY FLANK STEAK

Prep time: 15 mins • Cook time: 15 mins • 5-6 Servings
(at least 1 hour of hands off prep)

INGREDIENTS

- 3 Tbsp extra virgin olive oil
- 3 Tbsp freshly squeezed lime juice
- 1 Tbsp Dijon mustard (or wasabi powder)
- 1 garlic clove, minced (or 1 tsp garlic powder)
- 1 tsp ground cumin
- 1 tsp paprika
- 1 Tbsp chili powder
- 1 cup plain goat's milk yogurt
- 1 grass-fed flank steak (about 1 ¼ pounds)
- Sea salt to taste

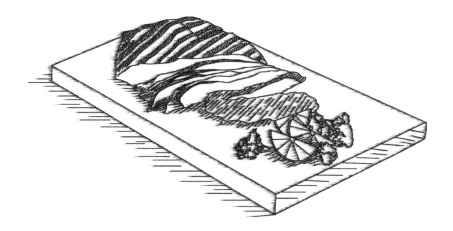

DIRECTIONS

1. Combine the following ingredients in a sealable plastic bag: oil, lime juice, Dijon mustard, garlic, cumin, paprika, chili powder, and yogurt. Seal bag and shake to mix well.

2. Add steak to bag. Make sure the meat is well coated in marinade and let marinate for AT LEAST one hour, or as long as 8.

3. When steak is done marinating, preheat a grill or skillet over high heat.

4. Remove steak from marinade, pat dry, and sprinkle with salt.

5. Cook to preferred temp (medium rare is about 4 minutes per side, cook longer if desired). Let rest for approx. 5 minutes before serving.

6. When slicing, make sure to slice steak against the grain.

7. Serve with roasted parmesan and garlic Brussels sprouts and cauliflower mash!

SPICY JICAMA
FRENCH FRIES

Prep time: 15-20 mins • Cook time: 1 houra • 4-5 Servings

INGREDIENTS

- 1 lb jicama, peeled and sliced into the shape of a French fry
- 3 tbsp ghee butter
- 1 tsp chili powder
- ½ tsp garlic powder
- ½ tsp onion powder
- ¼ tsp paprika
- ½ tsp cumin
- Black pepper and salt to taste

DIRECTIONS

1. Preheat oven to 400 degrees F.

2. Add water and jicama fries to a medium pot, boil for approx. 15 minutes.

3. Remove and pat dry.

4. Melt butter and combine with seasonings.

5. Toss jicama in seasoning mix and coat evenly.

6. Spread in a single layer on a baking sheet.

7. Bake for 20 minutes, flip them, and then bake for another 20 minutes.

8. Remove from oven when done. Let rest 3-4 minutes before serving.

SPINACH AND GOAT CHEESE SOUFFLÉ

Prep time: 20 mins • **Cook time: 40 mins** • **6 Servings**

INGREDIENTS

- 3 Tbsp parmesan cheese, grated
- 2 Tbsp ghee butter, melted
- 2 tsp avocado oil
- ½ lb breakfast sausage
- 10 oz fresh spinach, roughly chopped
- 1 ½ Tbsp garlic, minced
- ¼ cup yellow onion, finely diced
- 4 eggs with the yolks & whites separated (make sure room temp)
- 1 ½ - 2 cups soft goat cheese
- ½ cup heavy cream
- ¼ tsp black pepper
- ½ tsp salt, divided
- ½ Tbsp chives, finely chopped
- Red pepper flakes (optional)
- 3 Tbsp almond flour (very fine)

1. Preheat oven to 375 degrees F.

2. Use just enough of the melted butter to grease a 2qt soufflé dish. Save the remaining melted butter.

3. Sprinkle the parmesan cheese in the soufflé dish. Shake the dish until the bottom and sides are coated with the cheese. If any extra parmesan is at the bottom, remove it from the dish and save to use for topping.

4. Over medium-high heat, cook sausage until no longer pink, breaking apart with a wooden spoon as you stir. Once cooked through, set aside.

5. Heat olive oil in a non-stick pan over medium heat. Once hot, add the diced onions, minced garlic, and chopped spinach. Cook until spinach has cooked down and garlic and onions become fragrant, be sure to stir frequently.

6. Add ¼ tsp salt and continue to cook for another 2-3 minutes until the spinach is dry.

7. In a blender, place egg yolks, remaining salt and melted butter, heavy cream, goat cheese, black pepper, chives, red pepper flakes, and almond flour. Blend until creamy, scraping down sides as needed.

8. In a medium bowl, beat the egg whites until stiff peaks form. Make sure to not to stop too soon, it may take a little while until you see the peaks form.

9. In a large bowl, place the cooked spinach mixture with the egg yolk mixture. Stir together.

10. Next, CAREFULLY fold in the whipped egg whites. It is important that you are very gentle when folding them in, because the fluffy texture depends on this step.

11. Place mixture into the soufflé dish. Top with remaining parmesan and bake for 40 minutes, or until the top is nicely puffed up and golden.

12. Serve and enjoy!

STUFFED PORK LOIN

Prep time: 25 mins • **Cook time: 1 hour (or more)** • **5 servings**

INGREDIENTS FOR THE STUFFING

- 2 cups cooked millet
- ½ cup extra virgin olive oil
- ¼ cup fresh thyme, minced
- ¼ cup fresh parsley, minced
- 1 Tbsp fresh rosemary, minced
- 1 cup celery, diced

- 1 cup onions, diced
- 1 cup mushrooms, diced
- 1 cup Brussels sprouts, shredded
- 1 cup pistachios, shelled and coarsely chopped
- 1 Tbsp poultry seasoning (optional, you can add herbs/spices if you do not have this)

INGREDIENTS FOR THE PORK

- 1 pork loin (or pork crown rib roast)
- ¾ tsp sea salt
- ¾ tsp black pepper
- ½ cup extra virgin olive oil

- 5 cloves garlic, minced (divided)
- 1 Tbsp fresh thyme, minced
- ¼ cup fresh parsley, minced
- 1 cup balsamic vinegar (for the glaze)

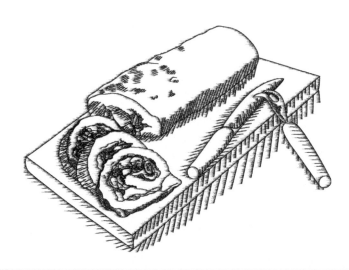

1. Preheat oven to 350 degrees F.

The Balsamic Reduction:

1. Pour 1 cup balsamic vinegar in a pan over low heat and cook until syrupy, stirring occasionally. Once it's syrupy, remove from heat and set aside. NOTE: you can make the stuffing while you are making this reduction.

The Stuffing:

1. Heat ¼ cup olive oil in a large skillet over medium heat. Once hot, add the celery and onions and cook until tender, approx. 5-6 minutes. Add the thyme, parsley, rosemary, poultry seasoning, and half of the garlic and cook until very fragrant. Set aside in a large bowl.

2. Pour additional ¼ cup of oil to the pan, and add the Brussels sprouts and mushrooms. Cook for 7-8 minutes on high heat, tossing occasionally. When done, add to the bowl with the onion mixture.

3. Add cooked millet and pistachios to the bowl and toss to combine. Taste and add salt and pepper if needed – let cool to room temperature before stuffing the pork.

Make the herb baste:

1. From the ingredients listed for the pork, combine the salt, pepper, garlic, thyme, and parsley. Set aside.

For the pork:

1. Cut your pork loin from one side of the loin to the other horizontally, stopping ½ inch from the end. Continue this process until you've made a deep pocket. Season with salt and pepper. NOTE: you can also cut it until the pork "unrolls" and opens like a book. You will spread the stuffing evenly on pork and then roll it up, using butcher's twine to hold it all together.

2. Place the stuffing mixture in the pork loin "pocket" and brush with the herb baste, using all of the herbs.

3. Bake on a lightly greased sheet tray for 45-60 minutes, until a thermometer inserted into the center of the stuffing reaches 165 degrees.

Finishing touches:

1. When the pork as reached the appropriate temperature, brush it with balsamic glaze and bake an additional 10 minutes. Then let rest for 10-15 minutes before serving.

2. Pair the pork with delicious cauliflower mac and cheese or cauliflower mash!

STUFFED SWEET POTATOES

Prep time: 10-15 mins • Cook time: 10 mins • 4 Servings

INGREDIENTS

- 2 sweet potatoes (medium)
- 1 tsp extra virgin olive oil
- 1 ¼ tsp cumin
- ¼ tsp salt
- ¼ tsp black pepper
- ¾ lb ground turkey (or ground beef)
- 4 cloves garlic, minced
- 1 tsp chili powder
- ½ tsp paprika
- ¼ cup Buffalo mozzarella cheese
- Toppings: sour cream, avocado, chopped scallions

1. Pierce the sweet potatoes all over with a fork. Cook in the microwave on HIGH until tender, approx. 4 - 5 minutes per side. Let the potatoes cool slightly.

2. Cut the potatoes in half, lengthwise. Carefully scoop the flesh out of the potatoes and place in a medium-sized bowl. Set the skins aside.

3. Mash the potato flesh with a fork until most lumps are gone.

4. Add the olive oil, ½ tsp cumin, salt, and pepper. Stir until combined.

5. Scoop the mixture into the skins, making sure to evenly distribute. Place on a cooking sheet.

6. Preheat the broiler.

7. While broiler is heating up, heat a nonstick skillet over medium-high heat (may need to lightly coat it with cooking spray).

8. Add the ground turkey and cook until cooked thoroughly and broken into crumbles.

9. Stir in the garlic, remaining cumin, paprika, chili powder, and additional salt and pepper if preferred. Cook for 1 minute.

10. Spoon the turkey mixture into each sweet potato skin. Top each with buffalo mozzarella cheese.

11. Broil until the cheese is melted, be careful not to burn.

12. Top with chopped scallions, avocado, and sour cream and enjoy!

SWEET ORANGE CHICKEN MEATBALLS

Prep time: 10 mins • Cook time: 30 mins • 4 Servings

INGREDIENTS

For the Meatballs

- 2 cloves garlic, minced
- 2 tsp avocado oil (olive oil or coconut oil are also acceptable)
- 4 large mushrooms, finely diced (to make approx. 1 cup diced)
- 1 lb ground chicken (NOT ground chicken breast)
- ¼ cup finely sliced scallions
- 1 tsp coconut aminos
- ½ tsp sesame oil
- 1 Tbsp orange zest
- ½ cup almond flour
- ½ cup coconut flour
- Dash of salt and pepper

For the Sauce

- 2 cloves garlic, finely minced
- 1 Tbsp ginger root, finely minced
- 2 tsp avocado oil
- 2 Tbsp coconut aminos
- 1 tsp sesame oil
- 1 Tbsp orange zest
- ½ tsp Sriracha
- 1 tsp tapioca starch
- ½ cup chicken stock
- ½ cup orange marmalade
- ½ - 1 Tbsp white wine vinegar

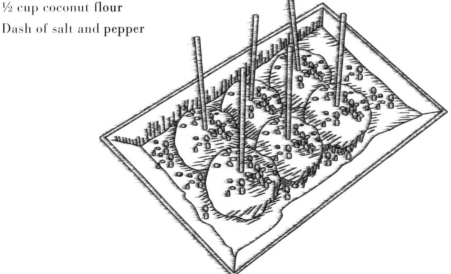

1. Preheat oven to 400 degrees F.

2. In a medium pan, heat avocado oil over medium-high heat.

3. Add garlic and sauté until fragrant, about 1 minute.

4. Add mushrooms and scallions and season with a dash of salt and pepper. Stir until mushrooms have released their liquid, approx. 3 minutes. Remove from heat and cool slightly.

5. In a large bowl, mix ground chicken, sesame oil, coconut aminos, orange zest, almond flour, coconut flour, and sautéed mushroom mixture with a wooden spoon.

6. With damp or lightly greased hands, take mixture and roll into balls. Should make about 18 meatballs.

7. Place meatballs on a parchment lined sheet and bake for 20 minutes.

8. While meatballs are baking, you can make the sauce: place a pan over medium high heat, add a Tbsp avocado oil, ginger, and garlic, allow to sauté until fragrant.

9. In a small bowl, whisk together remaining ingredients and pour into pan. Stir until sauce thickens slightly - about 3 minutes.

10. Once meatballs are done, add to the sauce and gently stir to coat. (Sauce should be thick).

11. Dish and serve topped with sliced scallions and additional orange zest for more flavor!

TACO PIE

INGREDIENTS

- 1 pound ground beef
- 1 packet taco seasoning
- 3 green onions thinly sliced
- 1 cup Mexican blend cheese finely shredded, quantity divided
- 4 large eggs
- 2/3 cup heavy cream
- ½ tsp salt
- 1 ripe avocado, diced
- Sour cream and chopped scallions

1. Preheat oven to 350° Fahrenheit.

2. Prepare a 9" pie pan by greasing with butter or spraying with coconut oil.

3. Heat a large skillet over medium high heat. When skillet is hot, add ground beef and cook until browned, stirring occasionally and breaking up with a wooden spoon.

4. Drain beef and add taco seasoning and cook for a few more minutes, mixing seasoning with the beef. Set aside and let cool.

5. In a medium mixing bowl, whisk together eggs and heavy cream. Stir in the green onions, 3/4 cup of the cheese, and the salt.

6. Stir prepared taco meat into the egg mixture. Pour this mixture into the greased pie pan. Sprinkle remaining cheese on top (or more if you prefer).

7. Place pie dish into preheated oven and bake for 35-45 minutes or until the top is brown and the pie is set.

8. Allow to cool for 5 minutes before serving.

9. Dish into bowls and top with diced avocado, chopped scallions, and sour cream. Serve with a side of cilantro-lime cauliflower rice and enjoy!

THAI ALMOND
BUTTER NOODLES

Prep time: 5 mins • Cook time: 5 mins • 2-4 Servings

INGREDIENTS

- 1 – 2 cups miracle noodles, cooked according to package
- 2 Tbsp onion, chopped
- 2 Tbsp green peppers, diced
- 1 Tbsp coconut oil
- 1 tsp toasted sesame oil, cold-pressed
- 2 Tbsp bone broth
- 3 Tbsp almond butter
- 1 Tbsp coconut aminos
- 1 tsp apple cider vinegar
- 2 tsp pure maple syrup
- 1-2 tsp chili powder

1. Prepare miracle noodles according to directions on package.

2. While noodles are cooking, heat coconut oil in a sauce pan over medium-high heat.

3. Sauté the onions and green peppers until they are soft, golden, and fragrant.

4. Reduce temperature to medium-low heat and add almond butter, coconut aminos, apple cider vinegar, maple syrup and chili powder and combine. Stir for approx. 2 minutes.

5. Remove from heat and stir in sesame oil.

6. Portion out your noodles and pour sauce on top, stir to coat noodles.

7. Top with diced scallions.

8. Serve with steamed broccoli and roasted chicken, enjoy!

THICK AND CREAMY CHICKEN SOUP

Prep time: 20 mins • Cook time: 1 hour • 6 Servings

INGREDIENTS

- 1.5 - 2 lbs boneless, skinless, chicken breast
- 2-3 Tbsp ghee butter or coconut oil
- 1 large head of cauliflower, washed, cored, and chopped
- 1 medium yellow onion, diced
- 4 celery stalks, chopped
- 4 cups bone broth
- 1 can full-fat coconut milk
- 2 garlic cloves, minced
- 1 ½ tsp parsley
- 1 tsp salt
- pepper to taste
- Toppings: sour cream, shredded cheese, chopped scallions, and bacon bits (either pre-made or cook yourself)

1. Preheat oven to 350 degrees F.

2. Sprinkle chicken with salt & pepper before placing in a glass baking dish.

3. Add ½ - 1 cup of broth into the dish and place in oven for 25-30 minutes, making sure internal temperature is 165 degrees F.

4. In a large pot, melt ghee butter or coconut oil over medium heat.

5. Add onion and celery on medium heat and sauté for 5-10 minutes until soft/translucent.

6. Add in the cauliflower and garlic. Cover and sauté for 10 minutes, stirring occasionally.

7. Mix in the remaining amount of bone broth, coconut milk, parsley, salt & pepper. Bring to a boil and then reduce heat to simmer, uncovered for 30 minutes.

8. While the soup is simmering, your chicken should be done. Make sure to check it with a meat thermometer and it should be at least 165 degrees F. Remove from the heat and let it cool. Then dice and set aside.

9. After the soup has finished simmering, either use an immersion blender, food processor, or regular blender to blend until a creamy consistency.

10. Return soup to pot and add in chicken. Let soup cook for another 5 minutes to heat it back up.

11. Ladle soup into bowls and garnish with sour cream, shredded cheese, scallions, and bacon bits. Enjoy!

TUNA SALAD

Prep time: 10-15 mins • **Cook time: no cooking!** • **4 Servings**

INGREDIENTS

For the Chipotle Sauce

- 1 egg
- ½ Tbsp brown mustard
- 2 tsp fresh lemon juice
- ½ tsp ground chipotle pepper
- 1 tsp smoked paprika
- ¼ tsp salt
- 1 tsp onion powder
- ¼ cup avocado oil
- ½ cup mayonnaise

For the Tuna Salad

- 2 (5 oz) cans solid white albacore tuna, drained
- 4 slices bacon, cooked until crisp, drained, and crumbled
- ½ medium avocado, diced
- ½ cup celery, diced
- ½ cup onions, diced
- ¼ cup chipotle sauce (recipe above)
- Scallions, chopped for garnish
- 8 slices gluten-free bread

1. For the chipotle sauce: in a medium bowl (recommend one with high sides), add egg, mustard, lemon juice, chipotle pepper, paprika, salt, onion powder, avocado oil, and mayonnaise. Use an immersion blender to emulsify ingredients. Once creamy, set aside or refrigerate.

2. For the tuna salad: in a large bowl, combine the albacore, crumbled bacon, onions, celery, and chipotle sauce (can start add more sauce as desired). Add in the diced avocado and stir.

3. Serve on gluten-free bread and pair with homemade sweet potato chips!

VEGGIE SUSHI

Prep time: 15 mins • Total time: 15 mins • 4 Rolls

INGREDIENTS

- 4 sheets seaweed
- 1 pound cucumbers, thinly sliced and peeled
- 1 ripe avocado, sliced into thin wedges
- 3 1/2 oz cooked chicken, cut into strips
- Coconut aminos, for serving
- Pink radishes, thinly sliced with a mandolin slicer
- Jicama (optional)

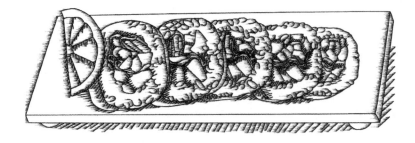

DIRECTIONS

1. Place a sheet of seaweed on a clean and dry cutting board, shiny side facing down and longest edge facing you.

2. Starting from the left edge, arrange the cucumber slices in overlapping rows, leaving a 3-cm (1-inch) margin of uncovered seaweed at the right.

3. Layer sliced radishes on top of cucumber.

4. Arrange the avocado in an even, vertical pattern, about 5 cm (2 inches) from the left edge

5. Rotate the cutting board by a quarter of a turn counter-clockwise so the uncovered strip of seaweed is furthest from you. Using both hands, start rolling the sheet from the edge closest to you, folding it up and over the fillings, then rolling it tightly.

6. Just as you're about to reach the uncovered strip of seaweed at the end, dip your fingertips in water and dab the sheet of seaweed lightly so it will stick.

7. Set aside, seam side down, and repeat with the remaining ingredients to make three more rolls

8. Slice into halves or thick slices using a sharp chef knife.

9. Serve with coconut aminos for dipping. Mix with wasabi powder for a nice kick!

SUPER SMOOTHIE

Prep time: 5 mins • Cook time: no cooking! • 1 Serving (1 Glass)

INGREDIENTS

- ½ avocado, pitted and peeled
- ½ cup vanilla coconut yogurt
- ¼ cup pear slices
- ¼ cup plums
- ¼ cup blueberries
- 1 handful of spinach
- 1 cup ice

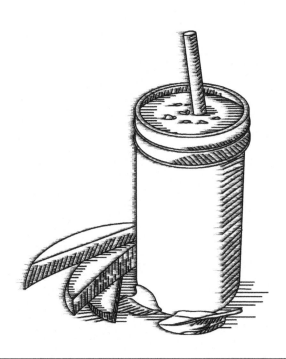

1. Place all ingredients in high powered blender.

2. Blend until smooth (add water if you have trouble blending it).

WARM APPLE CRISP WITH COCONUT MILK ICE CREAM

Prep time: 10 mins • **Cook time: 30 mins** • **6 Servings**

INGREDIENTS

- 4 cups apples, peeled & sliced/diced (do not make too small)
- 1 Tbsp Swerve
- 2 Tbsp water
- 1 tsp arrowroot
- 2 tsp ground cinnamon
- 1/8 – ¼ tsp nutmeg
- 1/2 cup almond flour
- 1/4 cup Stevia brown sugar
- 2 tsp ground cinnamon
- 2 Tbsp unsalted butter (place in freezer)

1. Preheat the oven to 350.

2. Coat a pie dish with cooking spray.

3. In a large bowl, toss together the apples, Swerve, water, arrowroot, 1 tsp cinnamon, and nutmeg until well combined. Set aside

4. In a food processor, add 1 tsp cinnamon, almond flour, and Stevia brown sugar and pulse until combined.

5. Remove butter from freezer and put into food processor and pulse (roughly until small chunks).

6. Place the apple mixture in the pie dish and sprinkle the topping evenly over the apples,

7. Bake for 25 - 30 minutes (until the apples are cooked through, the juices are bubbling, and the topping is browned).

8. Serve with a side of no sugar added coconut milk ice cream!

BERRY COCONUT CUPS

Prep time: 8 mins • **Cook time: 10 minutes** • **12 Servings**

INGREDIENTS

- 1 cup coconut cream concentrate
- 1 cup blueberries
- 1 cup coconut oil
- 1/3 cup raw honey
- ¼ cup unsweetened shredded coconut

1. Heat a small saucepan over medium heat.

2. Once hot, add blueberries and honey.

3. Mix until blueberries burst open, then add coconut cream concentrate and coconut oil.

4. Mix to combine thoroughly.

5. Remove from heat and add shredded coconut.

6. Place paper muffin liners into a muffin tin and pour mixture into each. How much you pour into each is up to you, depends on how big you wan t them to be!

7. Place in freezer for at least 20 minutes before consuming.

8. Keep the rest in freezer until you are ready to eat them!

NO BAKE
COOKIE DOUGH

Prep time: 10-15 mins • **Cook time: no bake!** • **8 Servings**

INGREDIENTS

- ¼ cup butter, softened
- ¾ cup Stevia brown sugar, packed
- ¼ tsp fine sea salt
- ¼ cup coconut milk
- 1 tsp pure vanilla extract
- ¾ cup almond flour
- ¾ cup coconut flour
- ½ tsp xanthan gum
- ½ cup carob chips or chopped dark chocolate (72% or greater)

1. In a medium bowl, add the butter, brown sugar, and salt. Mix with a hand mixer until smooth and creamy. Carefully mix in the milk and vanilla.

2. Gradually add the flour and xanthan gum and mix to completely combine.

3. Stir in the carob chips or dark chocolate.

4. Cover and refrigerate for 30 minutes.

5. After the dough has chilled, use a small scoop to form the dough into bite-sized balls.

6. Place on a plate covered in wax paper or plastic wrap and repeat with the remaining dough.

7. Cookie dough balls can be enjoyed as is or have with delicious coconut milk ice cream!

"CHOCOLATE CHIP" COOKIES

Prep time: 10 mins • Cook time: 10 mins • 18 Cookies

INGREDIENTS

- 2 Tbsp Stevia brown sugar
- 2 Tbsp Swerve
- 3 Tbsp coconut oil
- 1 large egg
- 1 tsp vanilla extract
- 1 tsp baking powder
- 2 cups almond flour, super fine (do not use almond meal)
- ¼ tsp salt
- ½ cup carob chips

1. Preheat oven to 375 degrees F.

2. Line a cookie sheet with parchment paper.

3. In a small bowl, mix the brown sugar, Swerve, and coconut oil until well combined.

4. With a fork, beat in the egg and vanilla extract.

5. In a medium bowl, stir together almond flour, baking powder, and salt.

6. Add wet ingredients to dry and stir with a wooden spoon. Add in carob chips. Stir to combine.

7. Spoon rounded tablespoons of cookie dough onto lined cookie sheet, approx. two inches apart.

8. Flatten dough slightly.

9. Bake for 10-11 minutes, or until the outsides of cookies begin to brown.

10. When done baking, let them cool and then transfer them to a cooling rack to continue to set.

11. Enjoy with no sugar added coconut milk ice cream!

CHOCOLATE RAZZ SMOOTHIE

Prep time: 5 mins • **Cook time: no cooking!** • **2 Servings**

INGREDIENTS

- 2 containers (5.3 oz. each) dark chocolate coconut almond dairy-free yogurt
- 1 cup coconut milk (may need more, but start with 1 and gradually add if needed)
- 1 cup raspberries
- 2-3 Tbsp ground flaxseeds
- 1 ripe banana
- 1 Tbsp carob powder
- Several ice cubes (optional)

1. Combine all ingredients in blender and blend on the smoothie setting, or until well blended.

2. Pour into one large or two small glasses.

3. Enjoy!

COCONUT AND MINT CHOCOLATE CHIP POPSICLES

Prep time: 10 mins • **Cook time: freeze 5 hours** • **6 Popsicles**

INGREDIENTS

- 1 cup coconut yogurt
- 1 ½ cup coconut milk
- 1 tsp pure vanilla extract
- ¾ tsp mint extract
- 2 Tbsp Swerve
- ½ cup carob chips, chopped
- Green Food Coloring, optional
- 6 Popsicle sticks

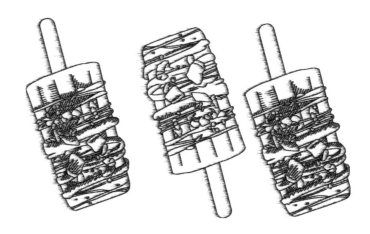

154

1. In a mixing bowl, add the yogurt, milk, vanilla, mint extract, chopped carob chips, and green coloring. Whisk mixture until thoroughly combined.

2. Pour the mixture evenly into popsicle molds.

3. Place sticks in the middle of the molds.

4. Place the mold in the freezer for at least 5 hours to freeze solid.

5. When ready to serve, run the base of the molds under hot water briefly and then grab the sticks and gently wiggle the pops out of the mold.

6. Enjoy!

COCONUT AND PISTACHIO CUPS

Prep time: 5-10 mins • **Freezing time: 60-80 mins** • **24 mini cups**

INGREDIENTS FOR CUPS

- 1 cup pistachios, roughly chopped
- 1 cup coconut oil, melted/liquid
- ¼ cup carob powder
- ¼ cup date nectar (see recipe below)
- ¼ cup almond butter
- 1 tsp vanilla bean powder
- Sea salt
- Whipped coconut cream
- Shredded coconut, toasted

INGREDIENTS FOR HOMEMADE DATE NECTAR

- 8-9 dates
- 1 ¼ cup water
- 1 ½ tsp lemon juice

DIRECTIONS FOR CUPS

1. Add all ingredients (except sea salt, whipped coconut cream, and shredded coconut) into a medium bowl and stir until well combined.

2. Pour mixture evenly into 24 mini-muffin cups.

3. Place the mini-muffin cups on a baking sheet, then transfer to the freezer for approximately 20 minutes, or just long enough for the tops to slightly harden.

4. Remove the baking sheet from the freezer and sprinkle sea salt on top of each of the fudge cups.

5. Return the baking pan to the freezer for approximately 30-60 minutes, or until they are firm all the way through (or to your preference).

6. Once they are hard, top with whipped coconut cream and toasted shredded coconut and enjoy!

DIRECTIONS HOMEMADE DATE NECTAR

1. Place the dates in a small bowl; cover entirely with warm water and let sit for 30 minutes.

2. Once the dates have soaked, drain the water then add the dates, 1-¼ cup water, and lemon juice to a high speed blender.

3. Blend for 45-60 seconds, or until smooth.

DARK CHOCOLATE AND COCONUT CAKE

Prep time: 15 mins • **Cook time: 30 mins** • **8 Servings**

INGREDIENTS

For the Cake

- ¼ cup coconut flour
- ¼ cup almond flour
- ½ tsp baking soda
- ½ tsp salt
- ¼ cup coconut milk, lite
- 6 eggs
- 1/3 cup honey
- ½ tsp apple cider vinegar
- 1-2 tsp pure vanilla extract

For the Frosting

- 1 cup coconut butter
- ½ - ½ cup pure maple syrup

For the Topping

- Shredded coconut, toasted
- 72% dark chocolate, shaved
- Walnuts, coarsely chopped

1. Preheat oven to 350 degrees F.

2. In a small bowl, combine both flours, baking soda, and salt.

3. In another bowl, beat the milk, honey, eggs, apple cider vinegar, and vanilla extract.

4. Add dry ingredients to wet ingredients, mix well.

5. Grease cake pan (bottom and sides) with butter or cooking spray.

6. Pour the batter into an 8 inch cake pan.

7. Bake for 25-30 minutes or when lightly browned.

8. For frosting: in a small bowl, mix coconut butter and maple syrup.

9. When the cake is cool, frost it and then add toppings.

10. Serve with a side of coconut milk ice cream and enjoy!

CHOCOLATE AND RASPBERRY COCONUT ICE CREAM

Prep time: 4 hours • **Cook time: no cooking involved!** • **10 Servings**

INGREDIENTS

- 2 avocados (pitted)
- 1 can (13.5 oz) full-fat coconut milk
- ½ cup carob powder
- ¼ cup pure maple syrup
- ½ tsp pure vanilla extract
- ¼ tsp sea salt
- 1 cup freeze-dried raspberries

For the topping
- ½ cup freeze-dried raspberries

DIRECTIONS

1. What you will need to prepare in advance: put your 13.5 ounce can of full-fat coconut milk in the freezer for 1 hour prior to making this recipe. You will be using only the "fat" part of the coconut milk, and not the "water". If you already have coconut in the back of the fridge, you can use that as well.

2. Remove the can of coconut milk from freezer or fridge and scoop out only the hardened coconut "fat" part, and add it to a high powered blender. Do not discard that water part of the coconut milk as this can be used for another recipe if you wish.

3. Add all the remaining ingredients for the ice cream to the blender and blend until it's creamy and smooth.

4. Add the 1 cup of add-in freeze-dried raspberries and gently stir them in by hand. Do not blend them.

5. Transfer the mixture to an 8x5 pan, lined with parchment paper and spread it evenly in the pan.

6. Add the 1/2 cup of topping freeze-dried raspberries evenly on the top of the ice cream mixture.

7. Put the pan in the freezer for approximately 2-3 hours, or until it hardens.

8. When ready to serve, remove from the freezer and cut into small square pieces or rectangle bar pieces. Store extras in the freezer in an air-tight container.

"CHOCOLATE" CHIP BARS WITH WHIPPED COCONUT CREAM

Prep time: 15 mins • Cook time: 30 mins • 12 Servings

(make sure to let coconut milk sit in fridge overnight)

INGREDIENTS FOR BARS

- ¼ cup coconut oil, melted
- 1/3 cup pure maple syrup
- 2 tsp pure vanilla extract
- 2 eggs, slightly beaten

- ¼ cup unsweetened coconut milk
- ½ cup coconut flour
- ½ tsp baking soda
- ¼ tsp salt
- 3 oz carob chips

INGREDIENTS FOR CREAM

- 1 can(13.5 ounce can) full-fat coconut milk (refrigerate overnight)
- 4 Tbsp Stevia blend
- 1-2 tsp pure vanilla extract

DIRECTIONS FOR BARS

1. Preheat oven to 350 degrees F.

2. Spray 8x8 inch baking pan with nonstick cooking spray.

3. In a large bowl, whisk together coconut oil, maple syrup, vanilla, eggs, and coconut milk.

4. In a separate medium bowl whisk together coconut flour, baking soda, and salt.

5. Add dry ingredients to wet ingredients and mix until just combined and batter is smooth.

6. Fold in carob chips, reserve a few tablespoons for sprinkling on top if desired.

7. Bake for 20-22 minutes (start with 20) or until edges are golden brown. Poke the center with a knife, you will know it is done when the knife comes out with a few crumbs attached. The batter may look like it's not all the way cooked but it will be. DO NOT OVERBAKE or it will result in dried out bars.

8. Cool bars on a wire rack for at least 10 minutes so that they set, then cut into squares and top with whipped coconut cream!

DIRECTIONS FOR CREAM

1. Remove the can of coconut milk from the refrigerator and open with a can opener. There should be a thick layer of coconut "fat" on the top of the can and coconut water on the bottom.

2. Carefully scoop out the coconut "fat" and add it to an electric mixer bowl. NOTE: save the coconut water at the bottom for a different recipe!

3. Add the Stevia and vanilla extract to the mixer bowl.

4. Mix on high until it becomes thick and peaks.

COCONUT AND CAROB HAYSTACKS

Prep time: 5 mins • Cook time: 20 mins • 12 Servings

INGREDIENTS

- 4.5 oz carob chips
- 2 Tbsp ghee butter
- 1 ½ cup unsweetened coconut flakes, toasted

DIRECTIONS

1. Preheat oven to 325 degrees F.

2. Spread coconut flakes on a baking sheet and bake for 3 minutes.

3. Once done, remove from oven and stir. Cook again for an additional 3 minutes or until coconut is browned.

4. Use a double broiler for this step. Pour water into pot and bring to boil and then turn heat down to simmer. Add carob chips and butter to the double broiler and stir until completely melted.

5. Add toasted coconut to melted carob and butter mixture, mix until coconut is fully covered.

6. Spoon mixture (approx. ½ - ¾ tsp at a time) to a clean sheet of parchment paper.

7. Set in freezer for 10 minutes and then place in the refrigerator.

8. Once hardened, remove and enjoy!

MINT CHOCOLATE DESSERT BARS

Prep time: 30 mins • Cook time: no cooking! • 12 Bars

INGREDIENTS FOR BOTTOM LAYER

For Mint Layer

- 1 avocado, peeled and pitted
- ¼ cup raw honey
- 6 Tbsp coconut oil, melted
- 1 ½ cup shredded unsweetened coconut
- 3/8 tsp mint extract
- Pinch of salt

INGREDIENTS FOR TOP LAYER

For Chocolate Layer

- ¼ cup coconut oil
- 2 Tbsp raw honey
- ¼ cup carob powder
- ¼ tsp pure vanilla extract
- Pinch of salt

For Mint Layer

1. Line a 9×9 inch baking dish with foil.

2. Place all ingredients in high powered blender or a food processor.

3. Blend until slightly chunky (or can blend until completely smooth if you prefer).

4. Smooth mixture into prepared dish and stick in the freezer.

DIRECTIONS FOR TOP LAYER

For Chocolate Layer

1. In small saucepan, melt coconut oil and honey over low heat.

2. Remove from heat and stir in remaining ingredients.

3. Pour over chilled mint layer and return to the freezer for about 15 minutes, or until the chocolate layer is hardened.

4. Remove from foil and cut into bars.

5. Store covered in the freezer.

Made in the USA
Las Vegas, NV
10 August 2021